The Monster Hunter's Handbook

⚜ The ⚜
Monster Hunter's Handbook

The Ultimate Guide
to Saving Mankind from
Vampires, Zombies, Hellhounds,
and Other Mythical Beasts

Ibrahim S. Amin

BLOOMSBURY

Published by Bloomsbury USA, New York
Distributed to the trade by Holtzbrinck Publishers

All papers used by Bloomsbury USA are natural,
recyclable products made from wood grown in well-managed forests.
The manufacturing processes conform to the environmental
regulations of the country of origin.

LIBRARY OF CONGRESS CATALOGING-IN-PUBLICATION DATA
HAS BEEN APPLIED FOR.

ISBN-10 1-59691-238-3
ISBN-13 978-1-59691-238-0

First U.S. Edition 2007

1 3 5 7 9 10 8 6 4 2

Typeset by Hewer Text UK Ltd, Edinburgh

Printed in China by South China Printing Co

❧ Contents ❧

Part II

To Heracles, the greatest of all time

⤜✧ Introduction ✧⤛

It is with great pleasure that I am finally able to present the wider public with two works contained within this volume. Previously they had only been made available to venerable institutions such as the Heraclean Club and the Mystical Blade Society—organizations specializing in either aggressive crypto-zoology or the search for, and acquisition of, legendary weapons. Now, however, a more general (albeit equally discerning, no doubt) readership will have access to the valuable information that they hold. With that in mind, it is perhaps worth taking a moment to explain the technical terms that appear in the two titles. While these will already be familiar to readers better acquainted with this subject matter, those new to the field may not necessarily have heard them before:

Cryptozoology: The study of creatures considered by the world at large to be mythical (e.g., vampires).

Cryptohoplology: The study of weapons and armor considered by the world at large to be mythical (e.g., Excalibur).

While they were originally conceived as separate works, there is no question that the two texts united within these covers complement each other rather well. *The Monster Hunter's Handbook: A Guide to Aggressive Cryptozoology* contains information on how the reader can slay various monsters with conventional weapons such as swords or firearms. However, the thought of attacking the more dangerous creatures with these meager tools, though an attractive proposition for sportsmen wishing to put their skills to the ultimate test, may be rather a daunting one for many people. For monster hunters desiring to acquire more powerful tools, to tilt the balance slightly more in their favor, *Enchanted Steel: A Guide to Cryptohoplology* should prove an adequate introduction to the field. This second work introduces some of the most prominent magical weapons and pieces of armor, which can be used to great effect when hunting the creatures contained within the first one.

Now read on, and step into the darkness that exists beyond the awareness of normal men. For the sooner you read these two works, the sooner you will be able to join us in the fight against monsters and the quest for legendary artifacts.

Part I
Monsters: A Guide to Aggressive Cryptozoology

Why Would Anyone Want to Hunt Monsters?

If you're standing in a bookstore or a library, and happen to have lifted this volume off the shelf out of general curiosity, the above question is probably swimming through your mind. Why would a person want to read this book? Why would a person want to learn how to hunt monsters?

Most monster hunters are motivated, at least in part, by sport. A hunter does not kill merely to pass the time. He does not kill out of idleness or boredom. A hunter kills to test himself against what nature has to offer, to see if his humble human mind and body can overcome the power, quickness, and savage cunning of the beasts. Thus a true hunter will wish to pit himself against the most challenging prey—creatures that will push him to the limit. Any fool with a gun can shoot a deer, but only the greatest of sportsmen will be able to overcome a Hydra.

However, even among the most dedicated sportsmen in the field there is also a second, and perhaps far more noble concern—no less lofty a goal than the protection and preservation of the human race. Since ancient times monsters have plagued mankind, slaughtering men and women, sometimes tormenting entire towns or villages. And throughout history men such as Heracles have risen to destroy these fearsome beasts, and bring an end to their evil. The dark shadows hold many terrors, and without monster hunters to battle against them they could engulf the entire world. Though he may hunt for sport, to test himself and earn great acclaim for his achievements, a monster hunter is participating in this millennia-old tradition through which the forces of darkness are kept in check.

Perhaps you have no interest in hunting, and are therefore thinking of putting this book back on the shelf. Doing that could cost you your life. Would you know what to do if a vampire burst into your home at night? Would you know how to defend your loved ones if you were walking through a forest and were suddenly attacked by a rampaging werewolf? Even if you do not plan to go searching for a monster, there is no guarantee that a monster will not come searching for *you*. Thus the information contained within these pages might well save your life one day.

A Note on the Entries

The monster entries are in alphabetical order. Each entry will begin with a description of, and general information on, the creature in question. It will then proceed to a discussion of how the creature might best be dispatched. A summary will follow for ease of reference, listing the dangers a creature presents to hunters, any particular weaknesses it may have, and, where relevant, the possible souvenirs that can be acquired from it afterward.

Each entry concludes with a brief list of selected sources, for those who wish to learn more about any of the creatures in this work. Knowledge is power, and the greatest hunters understand the most about their quarry.

Regarding Weapons

The entries in this work will instruct the reader how to slay monsters while armed with archaic weapons such as swords or bows. This focus on premodern armaments is quite deliberate, since skilled monster hunters generally prefer to use the arms of the legendary hunters of old. This is in part done to uphold tradition, to wield forged steel and crafted wood like those great men whose achievements they wish to emulate. It is also to ensure that each hunt provides a greater challenge. Firearms and other such modern creations are certainly effective tools, but to a sportsman they make the hunt somewhat too easy. Thus references to contemporary weapons will be sparing, used only when they might prove necessary against the more difficult monsters. However, a nonhunter who is reading this book to defend himself against a potential monster attack should, of course, feel free to adapt the material contained within these pages when necessary, and to substitute guns and explosives for the described tools at his own discretion.

Hunters wishing to adhere to the traditions of monster hunting but who require slightly more potent weapons may wish to consult the companion volume to this work: *Enchanted Steel: A Guide to Cryptohoplology*. The legendary weapons covered therein should prove adequate for even the most dangerous hunts.

✽ Basilisk ✽

Description

*The basilisk is a type of serpent indigenous to the northern parts of
Africa. Our earliest surviving account of the monster comes from
the ancient Roman writer Pliny the Elder, who cataloged a number
of fabulous beasts in his* Natural History. *The snake is usually not
more than twelve fingers long, and possesses a distinctive white
mark on its head that resembles a crown. Unlike other snakes, a
basilisk moves in a curious upright fashion rather than slithering
along with its entire body pressed against the ground.*

*A basilisk is a potentially dangerous quarry for hunters if it
is attacked at close range. Any creature that meets its gaze will
perish, meaning that those foolhardy enough to approach it from
the front run a serious risk. Unlike with the Gorgon (see page
48), there is no evidence that a reflection of the creature is safe
to look upon. Hence a hunter will have to be extremely
cautious, and cannot rely on a device such as a mirror to keep
him safe. In addition, the basilisk is among the most poisonous
of monsters. According to the ancient sources, anything it
touches or breathes upon will wither and die.*

Killing Methods

Due to its aggressive toxicity and fatal gaze, engaging in melee
combat with a basilisk is to be avoided at all costs. The creature
should ideally be killed from a distance. Hence a bow or a sling
would be a suitable weapon, though the creature's relatively small
size could make it a slightly difficult target at long range. Hunters
should therefore ensure that they have adequate archery or

slinging skills before attempting to attack a basilisk, lest the creature be able to close the distance after a missed shot and bring its terrible poison or gaze into play. Area-effect weapons such as Greek fire—a chemical mixture capable of burning violently even on the surface of water—could also provide a viable option, since the attacker would not have to look directly at the basilisk, but could simply hurl or fire the weapon in the general vicinity of the monster. However, opinions in the hunting community vary over whether the use of such archaic incendiary weapons is considered sporting. While they make use of only ancient or medieval technology, and hence are viewed more favorably than modern explosive devices, some complain that they are used as a substitute for skill—that flooding an area with flames is an unskilled hunter's alternative to striking true with an arrow.

Curiously, in Pliny's passage on basilisks he claims that they can be killed by exposure to weasels. Apparently the weasel's odor will destroy the basilisk, though the weasel will also die from exposure to the creature. This source suggests that a hunter could locate a basilisk's hole (marked by the way the ground around it has been poisoned) and throw a weasel into it. Though even if a hunter wishes to adopt this approach, bringing along a bow or other such weapon would be a wise precaution in case the weasel succumbs to the basilisk's poison before killing it.

The basilisk's devastating poison might make a useful weapon if acquired after the beast's death. Obviously hunters wishing to collect this venom would have to be rather careful to avoid exposure to it.

⛤ Summary ⛤

Dangers

- Death-bringing stare
  - Poison

Weakness

- Weasels

Souvenir

- The creature's venom

Selected Source

Pliny the Elder. *Natural History* **8.33**. The earliest surviving description of the basilisk, its properties, and its vulnerability to weasels. Although Pliny was a Roman, his work is based on earlier (now lost) Greek sources.

❧ Centaur ❧

Description

Centaurs are creatures with the upper body of a man and the lower body of a horse. Thus they possess four powerful equine legs, enabling them to gallop at a fast rate and lash out with devastating kicks from their hooves. They can first be found in ancient Greek sources, which record that they often came into conflict with the legendary heroes of that age. A centaur once tried to abduct Heracles' wife, for example, and for this earned an agonizing death from the hero's poisoned arrows.

They are not mindless monsters, but are tool-using creatures with intelligence equal to that of men. They wield weapons and attack with skill rather than animalistic fury. Unlike many creatures, they also can fight in organized groups. This is perhaps best illustrated by their battle with Caeneus, a Greek hero whose skin was impenetrable to spears or swords. Seeing that they could not rend his flesh, the centaurs piled tree trunks on top of him, until he was buried and thus unable to breathe.

Killing Methods

Centaurs can be killed with conventional weapons, either at close quarters or from a distance. Both their human upper body and equine lower body are vulnerable to blades or arrows. However, they are dangerous opponents, and an engagement with large numbers of them is likely to resemble a full-scale battle rather than a hunt.

While skillful with weapons, even unarmed centaurs are not to be attacked without due caution. In addition to their powerful hooves, which can break bones and shatter skulls, they are proficient grapplers. In the famed sculptures known as the Parthenon Marbles, a centaur can be seen entangling a human antagonist's leg with his equine forelegs, lifting this limb into the air to put the human off balance while the centaur strangles him.

Centaurs are worthy opponents, and one of the few monsters that can be engaged in a true battle, to see which side will win after a grueling clash of arms. Hunters should relish such an opportunity to truly test their martial prowess.

Although victory against centaurs is largely a matter of possessing superior fighting skills rather than following a particular strategy or exploiting a specific weakness, there are certain tactics a hunter could use to help tilt the odds in his favor. For example, at close quarters centaurs should ideally be attacked from a flank, rather than directly from the front or behind. This should prevent them from kicking, since equine legs do not enjoy the same range of movement as human legs, and cannot be thrust to the side. To further limit a centaur's maneuverability and combat effectiveness, a hunter may wish to hamstring them.

❧ Summary ❧

Dangers

- Intelligent, tool-using creature
  - Hooves

Weakness

- Highly vulnerable to flank attacks

Selected Sources

Apollodorus. *Library* **2.7.6.** A description of how the centaur Nessus attempted to violate Heracles' second wife, Deianira, and was slain by the hero.

Ovid. *Metamorphoses* **12.210–535.** An account of the battle between centaurs and Lapiths, including the centaurs' burying of Caeneus—whose body could not be pierced.

❧ Chimera ❧

Description

The Chimera is a curious hybrid creature, first described in ancient Greek texts. It can best be envisioned as a lion, but with a snake in place of its tail and the head of a goat mounted atop its back. This goat's head can breathe fire. Unlike normal lions, there is no indication that the Chimera dwells in a pride alongside others of its kind. Instead it stalks alone, killing those who have the misfortune to encounter it.

The Greek hero Bellerophon is said to have killed such a beast by flying above it atop a Pegasus and shooting it with arrows.

Killing Methods

Despite its fearsome appearance, the Chimera is not difficult to kill. As the encounter with Bellerophon illustrates, a hunter can simply bring the creature down with his bow. Any ranged weapon would be ideal against this particular monster.

Fighting a Chimera at close quarters, however, is not a good idea. As it possesses the head and body of a lion, it can use that animal's lethal teeth and claws to maul and rend unwary hunters. And although the goat's head atop its back may seem comical, such amusement will surely end when it breathes torrents of flame to char the flesh of its victims. In addition, the great serpent that makes up its tail has fangs that promise to add their bite to the leonine jaws when the Chimera pounces on a hunter who has recklessly strayed too near.

Even the mighty Bellerophon decided to battle the Chimera from the air, realizing how dangerous the beast would be if he drew too close. Thus he took to the skies atop a Pegasus, and dispatched the Chimera from a safe position. Hunters with access to such a fabulous mount may wish to emulate him.

❧ Summary ☙

Dangers

- Lion's teeth and claws
- Fire-breathing goat's head
- Serpent tail, possibly venomous

Weakness

- Vulnerable to conventional weapons

Souvenir

- A rather unique pelt

Selected Source

Apollodorus. *Library* 2.3.1–2. Description of the Chimera and Bellerophon's slaying of the beast.

✥ Cyclops ✥

Description

A Cyclops is a huge creature, resembling a human being but for its great size and single eye. Cyclopes tend to dwell on islands with others of their kind, preying on ships and travelers unfortunate enough to enter their domains. Though savage and brutish in their behavior, these monsters have some understanding of agriculture. They often keep flocks of sheep, and their caves contain stores of cheese and other such products. However, they will always dine on human meat when the opportunity arises.

The most famous Cyclops was undoubtedly Polyphemus, who captured Odysseus and his comrades on their voyage home from the Trojan War. This encounter ended badly for Polyphemus, after Odysseus offered him a particularly potent wine and blinded him while he lay in a drunken stupor. The Ithacan hero had previously managed to convince Polyphemus that his name was "No One," causing the blinded Cyclops to yell out that "No One" had harmed him—leading the other Cyclopes who had heard his screams of pain to believe that he was merely ill rather than under attack. If this incident is in any way an accurate reflection of the species, it appears that Cyclopes are not of high intelligence.

Killing Methods

Due to the huge size and devastating strength of Cyclopes, only a foolhardy hunter would attempt to engage one in close combat. Such an individual would no doubt quickly find himself seized, killed, and devoured by these creatures, who love to feast on human flesh.

To kill a Cyclops, a hunter should employ ranged weapons such as bows or slings, perhaps poisoning his missiles so they may more easily bring down such a large creature. However, Cyclopes often hurl boulders at their enemies. Hence hunters should not consider themselves beyond danger simply because they attack a Cyclops from a distance. It is advisable for a skilled hunter to target a Cyclops's eye first, to render the monster blind and therefore hamper its ability to accurately return fire.

In an emergency, a person forced to deal with a Cyclops may wish to exploit the creature's lack of intelligence by deceiving him. A small dose of poison placed in a tempting supply of wine might be an appropriate stratagem, for example.

❧ Summary ❧

Danger

- Immense size and power

Weakness

- Low intelligence

Selected Source

Homer. *Odyssey* **9.166–566.** An account of Odysseus's encounter with the Cyclops Polyphemus.

᠂᠊᠆ᢁ᠅ Djinn ᢁ᠅᠆

Description

*Djinn are humanoid creatures created from fire, and first appear
in ancient Arabic and Hebrew writings. While they vary considerably
in power and appearance, like most orders of spirits or demons,
even the lowliest members of the species are a difficult quarry.
Djinn can become invisible and intangible, rendering them almost
impossible to slay. Were this not enough of an impediment in
hunting them, powerful djinn also can change shape or grow to
immense size. Thus djinn are tremendously dangerous foes. They
are intelligent creatures rather than mindless beasts and hence
may make good tactical use of their powers to frustrate or even
slaughter unprepared hunters.*

*Hunters should be aware that djinn are not necessarily evil.
While some are indeed malign, others are not. In fact, some
apparently worship God and live pious lives. Solomon is said to
have had many God-fearing djinn at his side. Therefore hunters
may wish to be selective in which djinn they attack. Benign
djinn could potentially make useful allies, and have been
known to aid humans in a variety of ways. There are tales of
djinn building temples at the behest of human beings, leading
fishermen to places where they can make the best catches, and
sharing their treasure.*

Killing Methods

For all their supernatural powers, it does appear that djinn can be
killed. In some Arab folktales djinn express their fear that a mighty
prophet such as Solomon will slay them. The question is whether

this can be achieved through conventional means, via arrows and blades, or only by tapping into divine forces. Hunters should therefore have their weapons blessed before hunting for djinn, and perhaps even have them inscribed with passages from scripture. This should enable the weapons to be effective against djinn in either case.

Hunters may wish to avoid using incendiary weapons against djinn. Since djinn were supposedly created from intense fire, they may be resistant to this element. Of course, this may not necessarily be the case. According to similar beliefs, man may have been formed from clay, but a human being can still be killed by a blow from a heavy ceramic ashtray. Also, despite their fiery origins, djinn are not vulnerable to water. Sources describe members of the species living at the bottom of wells, or under the ocean. Even if they are formed from flame, and perhaps have some domain over fire, it does not appear that they can be extinguished.

A weakness of djinn is that they are rather arrogant and fond of vulgar displays of power. A cunning hunter can turn this against them. For example, one source recounts how a fisherman challenged a djinn to return to the jar in which he had previously been trapped, declaring that the djinn was surely not powerful enough to reduce his size to such a great degree. The foolish djinn attempted to demonstrate the extent of his powers by entering the jar, at which point the fisherman replaced the lid (which contained a holy inscription), binding him there. So even an unarmed person suddenly confronted by a djinn could make his escape if he effectively manipulated the creature in such a way. In addition, if a djinn can be bound to an object, it might be possible to bind it to a weapon, thereby increasing its killing power. The weapon would have to be inscribed with religious symbols or text, to hold the djinn in place, and the hunter would be taking a great risk in attempting this. As mentioned above, djinn are intelligent creatures, capable of meeting trickery with trickery, and wriggling out of any loophole with which they are provided.

When faced with a djinn that becomes intangible, and obstinately refuses to take on a physical form and be killed, a hunter with an expendable companion could attempt to have that companion possessed. As with other kinds of demon, there are numerous tales of people being possessed by djinn. For example, some folktales suggest that anyone unfortunate enough to urinate under a tree where an invisible djinn is sleeping will be possessed by the creature. A hunter wishing to use this stratagem should bring a great supply of liquid refreshment on a hunt, have his companion drink as much as possible, and persuade him to relieve himself under every suitable tree until he is possessed.

❧ Summary ❧

Dangers

- Magical powers
  - Possession

Weaknesses

- Arrogance
- Holy objects (?)

Souvenirs

- The wish-granting djinn itself
  - Treasure

Selected Sources

Burton, Richard, trans. *The Arabian Nights: Tales from a Thousand and One Nights.* **New York: Modern Library, 2001, 25–31.** A tale of how a fisherman encountered a murderous djinn, tricked him into returning to his jar, and ultimately made the creature help him.

Landa, Gertrude, *Jewish Fairy Tales and Legends.* **New York: Bloch, 1919, 80.** An account of how a djinn who dwelled at the bottom of a well gave a girl jewels.

Quran 15.27, 55.15. A description of djinn as being created from intensely hot, smokeless fire.

——— **27.17.** A description of Solomon's host, which contained both men and djinn.

⚜ Dragon ⚜

Description

Dragons are large reptilian creatures. Beyond that, however, they vary considerably in nature. There are numerous different breeds of dragon attested to in the historical source material. Since these present differing threats and challenges to hunters, the major variations must all be discussed here, so that a hunter will be well prepared for whichever type he faces. This entry will focus on the forms of dragon described in Western accounts. The dragons featured in Eastern texts differ wildly from those discussed below, and are often of a divine nature rather than being mere monsters.

Let us first address the nonwinged varieties of dragon. These may be divided into two distinct groups: those that dwell on land, and those that swim in the depths of the sea. Of the latter, an excellent description of a sea dragon is provided in the biblical accounts of Leviathan. The oceanic dragon is said to possess supremely resistant scales, which can withstand attacks from most weapons. Sea dragons also can breathe fire. This, of course, greatly increases the potential danger of the monsters, and hunters should be prepared to wear flame-retardant clothing.

Nonwinged land-dwelling dragons come in two varieties. The first is the "behemoth" dragon, named after the example of the breed chronicled in the Bible. This form of land-dwelling dragon possesses a similar physical hardiness to Leviathan. It is said that only God Himself could harm it with a sword. Unlike Leviathan, Behemoth is not described as being able to breathe fire. This dragon is apparently herbivorous. Therefore it may not possess the same reflexes and quick savagery that tend to be present in nature's carnivores.

The second of these wingless, land-dwelling breeds is the

cadmian, first attested to in ancient Hellenic sources. This type of dragon is named after the Greek hero Cadmus, who fought and killed such a monster prior to founding the city of Thebes.

Cadmians do not possess the heavy armor of the behemoth. While their tough hides are fairly resilient, they can be pierced by human might. However, they are swift, dangerous foes. They have been known to crush unwary attackers in their coils, and can expel poisonous fumes from their mouths. Curiously, the teeth of a cadmian dragon are said to yield a crop of fully grown, armed, and armored warriors if sown into a freshly plowed field. This would be a useful means of acquiring a squad of expendable retainers for future hunts.

Winged dragons, though made more fearsome by their ability to fly across the land, bringing devastation to vast swaths of countryside, are fortunately more akin to the cadmian than the behemoth. A heavily armored creature such as a behemoth or a sea dragon would be hard pressed to lift its weight into the air. Hence the winged breed is less well protected, with lighter scales.

They can breathe fire, however, like the sea dragon.

Dragons are among the most dangerous of monsters, and as such they are highly sought after by skilled monster hunters wishing to undergo the ultimate challenge and thus establish a reputation in the field. However, hunting these creatures can also provide more tangible rewards. Dragons are often described as sleeping in lairs filled with valuable treasures. Hence hunters may wish to locate the monster's domain after it has been dispatched, in the hope of acquiring great riches. They could also harvest the beast's armored scales, and employ them in crafting armor for future hunts. Such equipment would provide excellent protection and act as a trophy of one's achievements—making it eminently suitable attire in the company of other hunters.

Killing Methods

Let us consider each form of dragon in the order described above, beginning with the sea dragon.

The sea dragon is a fearsome quarry, combining great power with the ability to strike unexpectedly from the vast depths of the ocean. It is extremely difficult to kill, since according to the biblical account its scales can effortlessly resist the impact of swords, spears, javelins, clubs, arrows, and slings. For this reason, most segments of the monster-hunting community are willing to accept the use of modern weapons against these creatures. High-powered rifles are widely considered to be fair game, and some hunters with appropriate connections have even been known to use shoulder-fired rockets on dragon hunts. If a hunter is willing to use modern technology against a sea dragon, he might also consider discharging a large amount of electricity into the water around the monster in the hope that the resultant shock would kill it, depending on how much insulation its scales provided.

However, some hunting organizations, such as the prestigious Heraclean Club, insist that traditional weapons be used if a dragon hunt is to be considered a legitimate demonstration of one's hunting prowess. Thus if a reader desires to one day truly stand undisputed alongside the greats of the monster-hunting world, he must learn how to slay a dragon under these difficult conditions. One possibility would be for an enterprising hunter to employ some form of archaic chemical weapon such as Greek fire against the creature. This might be able to turn the waters around the beast into an inferno sufficiently powerful to destroy it. Alternatively, a hunter skilled in archery and with access to an especially virulent poison such as Hydra's blood could attempt to fire poisoned arrows into the dragon's eyes—which are presumably not armored, unlike the rest of the creature's body.

In terms of land-dwelling dragons, the behemoth would provide a similar challenge to the sea dragon. If it is true that only God could pierce the eponymous Behemoth's hide with a sword, then hunters lacking divinity would undoubtedly find their arrows and blades turned aside from the beast's armored flesh. However, as with the sea dragon, its eyes are probably the behemoth's one weak spot. Therefore a hunter wishing to employ traditional weapons, rather than attempting to test if powerful modern weapons could emulate God's sword in piercing a behemoth dragon's hide, would be well served to direct poisoned arrows at the beast's eyes. Alternatively, since the behemoth dragon walks on land, it could perhaps be approached at close quarters and charged—something that would be impossible with a sea dragon, since it would be surrounded by water. An especially brave or reckless hunter could in theory attempt to plunge a long weapon such as a pike through the creature's eye and into its brain—possibly charging from horseback to achieve greater momentum. Such a kill would unquestionably earn the hunter great acclaim from his peers, though the attempt could, of course, earn him nothing more than a painful death. If a reader does desire to attack a dragon in such a fashion, he could increase his chances of survival by arranging a distraction for the beast, so that he might attack while its attention is diverted. Given dragons' common tendency to amass treasure, it is possible that they can, like magpies, be distracted by shiny objects. Quantities of gold and silver could be used for this purpose.

The cadmian dragon is far less hardy than either the behemoth or the sea dragon. Though its hide can resist crushing damage from boulders or maces, sharp spears or swords wielded in strong hands will pierce its body. The hero Cadmus was able to slay the dragon he encountered with bladed weapons, so a skilled hunter should be able to do the same. Even so, hunters may prefer to keep their distance and rely on arrows, to avoid the poisonous breath these dragons possess. They may also wish to do this lest they be crushed in the creature's coils, which dragons are known to use in much the same way as a python. If undeterred by these risks, and wishing to face the beast at close quarters, hunters could emulate John Lambton. He is said to have worn armor covered with blades when battling the creature remembered in English folklore as the Lambton Worm. These blades tore the monster apart when it attempted to coil itself around him.

As mentioned above, winged dragons are more like the cadmian than the behemoth or the sea dragon, since such heavy armor would prevent them from taking flight. Thus legends abound with tales of winged dragons having their underbellies pierced by the swords and lances of great heroes. However, a hunter wielding a sword or a lance will face the problem of getting a winged dragon to the ground so he can bring his weapons to bear. Fortunately, a winged dragon's wings will probably be quite vulnerable, as heavy plating would hamper flight. Hence a hunter could shred the dragon's wings with slings, arrows, and spears should it come in range. If the dragon is flying too high, beyond the reach of such weapons, then it could perhaps be lured closer to the ground through the method of distraction suggested above—the use of shiny objects as bait.

Summary

Dangers

- Teeth
- Claws
- Poisonous/flaming breath

Weaknesses

- Unprotected eyes
- Soft underbelly, in the case of the winged dragon

Souvenirs

- Scales for armor
- Teeth
- Treasure

Selected Sources

Beowulf 2200–2820. A description of the winged dragon that ravaged Beowulf's kingdom, and his battle with it.

Henderson, William. *Notes on the Folk-Lore of the Northern Counties of England and the Borders.* **London: W. Satchel, Peyton, 1879, 287–89.** The tale of the Lambton Worm.

Ovid. *Metamorphoses* **3.28–130.** An account of how Cadmus killed a dragon with his spear and sowed its teeth to produce a crop of armed men.

Psalm 104.25–26; Job 40.15–24, 41.1–34. Descriptions of Leviathan and Behemoth.

⊱ Fairy ⊰

Description

Fairies are mischievous beings of varying humanoid shape. There are numerous different varieties of fairy folk, ranging from petite winged sprites to grotesque goblins, or slender creatures that stand taller than a man. Though fairies are often thought of as benign creatures by society at large, Celtic folklore is filled with tales of fairies stealing babies and causing harm to mankind. Thus they can justifiably be labeled monsters, though they may sometimes wear pleasant appearances of great contrast to many of the other beasts that populate this work.

Fairy folk usually possess magical powers, and are especially known for weaving illusions. A common tactic of theirs is to conjure up a false image of gold to entice their victims.

Killing Methods

Due to the vast physical differences among different types of fairy, the physical danger they present will depend on which particular fairy one happens to encounter. The larger breeds will perhaps be able to hold their own in open battle, whereas the smaller ones will rely more on trickery and guile. Fairies are masters of misdirection, employing enchantments to beguile the senses. A hunter must therefore be focused on his quarry, and not allow himself to become distracted by the illusions they may conjure up. Single-minded pragmatism is necessary for those who would slay fairy folk. Even if great riches and other such enticements seem to appear, the hunter must ignore these and go for the kill.

Fairies are particularly vulnerable to iron weapons. The slightest wound from such objects will cause great harm to them. Hence hunters may wish to resort to this more primitive metal, rather than using weapons of steel. Steel does, of course, contain iron, but its power could be diluted by the mixture, and therefore be less effective. However, in an emergency a little iron would obviously be better than none at all. Thus a steel sword or knife should be considered preferable to a graphite arrow or a wooden club, for example. As an absolute last resort, if a hunter finds himself wounded in battle with a fairy he might consider splashing the creature with his blood. While the iron content in human blood is not likely to cause any significant damage to a fairy, it may prove sufficient to provide a momentary distraction, enabling flight or a counterattack.

⚜ Summary ⚜

Danger

- Illusionary magic

Weakness

- Iron

Souvenir

- Treasure (though this is more often than not illusionary)

Selected Source

Sikes, Wirt. *British Goblins: Welsh Folk-lore, Fairy Mythology, Legends and Traditions.* **London: Samson Low, 1880.** A collection of folktales concerning fairies. Unfortunately, most recorded tales concerning these creatures have been collected and retold in a manner designed to entertain children rather than supply hunters with serious information. Nevertheless, such treasuries of tales can provide useful knowledge for those who might hunt the fairy folk, and thus desire to know about their powers and weaknesses.

⤜ Ghoul ⤛

Description

The term ghoul *is applied to various humanoid creatures that devour the corpses or even the live flesh of men, and the creatures appear in writings from many different cultures. Some ghouls are little more than insane or evil humans who have been corrupted. Others are demons that merely resemble humans, or undead creatures similar to vampires—once true men and women, but now sinister mockeries of life.*

Ghouls can usually be found where there is an abundance of corpses on which they can feed. Obviously places of burial are common environments for ghouls, especially if there are suitable crypts in which they can lurk and sleep during the day. However, battlefields have also been known to attract ghouls—eager to consume the flesh of dead heroes and cowards alike. Sites where accidents are common—for example, beneath treacherous cliff paths, or darkened roads where frequent crashes occur—may also be favorite haunts of ghouls.

Ghouls are often solitary monsters, but groups of the creatures can sometimes be found hunting and feasting together.

Killing Methods

When facing a human ghoul, the matter is rather simple. Any blade, arrow, bludgeon, or even bone-crunching wrestling hold could be used to dispose of the vile creature. Against an undead ghoul, on the other hand, a hunter would have to be careful to inflict severe destruction on the monster's body—lest it simply recover from a supposedly mortal wound and continue to present a threat. Destroying the ghoul's brain should suffice. Demonic ghouls are most likely from the lower orders of the demonic races. Surely powerful infernal beings would not lower themselves to lurking around graveyards and feasting on the rotting flesh therein. Even so, one should exercise a little caution, and perhaps bring along holy objects to defend against any unexpected dark powers the ghouls may possess.

While ghouls may not seem the most worthy prey for a skilled monster hunter, one must bear in mind that their disgusting habit of desecrating the dead is an insult to civilized society. Therefore slaughtering the repugnant beings would be a great public service. At the very least, those new to the field of monster hunting may wish to make ghouls their first targets. Of course, in the case of human ghouls a hunter must be aware of the legal ramifications of a successful hunt. Though few decent citizens would lament the deaths of foul men and women who cannibalize the bodies of their fellows, in purely legal terms killing ghouls may be considered murder.

Given their frequent interaction with corpses, ghouls are no doubt swarming with germs and disease. Hunters may therefore wish to keep their distance, and perhaps even use incendiary weapons such as flame-tipped arrows or Greek fire to ensure the total obliteration of the ghouls' unclean forms. If using close-combat weapons, these arms should be properly cleansed and disinfected after the hunt. The same should be done with any clothing that has come into contact with the creatures. While wading through a pack of ghouls, hewing off limbs and heads left and right may seem glamorous and noble, there is nothing glamorous about infection. At all costs hunters should avoid being bitten by ghouls. Even a normal human being's saliva is a potent biological weapon capable of causing great damage via an untreated bite. How much more damaging would the saliva of a creature that feeds on rotting corpses then be? In the event of a ghoul bite, immediate medical attention should be sought.

❧ Summary ❧

Dangers

- Disease
- Demonic powers (occasionally)

Weakness

- Limited strength and agility in some cases

Selected Source

Summers, Montague. *The Vampire*. London: Senate, 1995, 231–37. An account of various tales concerning ghouls.

⋙ Golem ⋘

Description

Golems are humanoid creatures made of clay, animated by ancient Hebrew magic. They are produced through a Kabbalistic ritual, during which a piece of paper containing the name of God is placed within them to provide a constant source of eldritch energy. This item can usually be found in the monster's mouth, arm, or where a man's heart would be.

During medieval times Jewish communities occasionally created golems to protect them against persecution by their enemies. However, golems were sometimes known to malfunction, and become a danger to all human beings—even those who created them.

Though a golem could presumably be made in any size or shape, most golems seem to be of approximately human form and dimensions. Yet since they are powered by supernatural means rather than being constrained by the limitations of muscle and bone, golems will likely possess strength well beyond that of a man.

Killing Methods

The methods via which a golem's body may be destroyed will vary somewhat, depending on whether its clay is soft or hard. If hard, crushing weapons such as warhammers or maces would perhaps be suitable for smashing it apart. If soft, cutting weapons such as swords or axes would be preferable to slice it to pieces. In either case, close combat is necessary, as arrows would be rather useless at destroying the golem's body.

Hunters wishing to conduct a more skillful kill, rather than one based on brute force, may wish to target the golem's "mind" rather than taking apart its body; in other words, the piece of paper or scroll inscribed with the Hebrew name of God. Once this is removed, the golem will cease to function. Should hunters ever find themselves in combat with a golem, and not have suitable weapons at hand with which to smash or dismember it, targeting this power source would be recommended.

Hunters should remember that a golem is essentially a piece of machinery. Thus eliminating a golem that is performing its legitimate duties would be little different from breaking a dishwasher or a microwave—an act of pure vandalism rather than a true hunting activity. Hence hunters should be careful to target only rogue golems that have become a danger to society.

❧ Summary ☙

Dangers

- Relentless and immune to pain
  - Supernatural strength

Weakness

- Requires the name of God to function

Selected Sources

Babylonian Talmud: Sanhedrin 65b. The earliest account of a golem being created.

Idel, Moshe. *Golem: Jewish Magical and Mystical Traditions on the Artificial Anthropoid*. Albany, N.Y.: State University of New York Press, 1990. A compilation and analysis of golem tales from ancient times onward.

⤞⅊ Gorgon ⅊⤝

Description

Gorgons are winged women with snakes for hair, and either tusks or fangs. They slay their victims merely by gazing upon them, for anyone who meets a Gorgon's stare will die.

According to the ancient Greek sources in which they are first recorded, there are two types of Gorgon: mortal and immortal. Naturally this is of great concern to hunters, since attempting to kill an immortal creature would be a rather pointless use of one's time. Unfortunately, the two types may well display the same physical characteristics; hence a degree of trial and error may be required. If the target one has attacked is in fact an immortal Gorgon, a hasty withdrawal would no doubt be advisable.

The Greek hero Perseus made his name as a monster hunter by slaying the Gorgon Medusa, and in doing so became one of the greatest of all Greek heroes. Though he attacked Medusa while she slept, perhaps to prevent her from taking flight and becoming more difficult to lay hands on, his deed is still considered one of the great milestones in monster hunting.

Killing Methods

In terms of the actual dealing of death, it seems to be no great challenge to slay a Gorgon. The ancient sources prescribe decapitation as a suitable method. Significantly, one source suggests that Perseus killed Medusa by grabbing the snakes that made up her hair, and then tearing her head off. This possibly indicates two things. First, the snakes are not poisonous and thus can be safely handled. Second, mortal Gorgons may have exceptionally weak necks. Yet it must be remembered that Perseus was a mighty hero. Perhaps pulling off people's heads was less unusual for such a man.

While Gorgons may be immensely killable, hunting them does carry certain risks. The major obstacle is that they have perfected the withering glare so commonly employed by women. A Gorgon's stare will petrify anyone who looks directly upon the creature's face, turning flesh and blood into cold stone. Indirect eye contact is apparently safe, as Perseus looked at Medusa's reflection on his shield when killing her. Hence a mirror or other well-polished surface would be useful when fighting Gorgons. In an emergency, any nearby bodies of water could possibly be used for this purpose. Attacking a Gorgon from behind could also be a viable option.

Those hunters who prefer to fight from range must be careful not to lock eyes with the Gorgon, even from a great distance. The scope of this monster's deadly gaze has never been established, and it is possible that meeting the creature's stare will bring death even from hundreds of feet away.

In addition to their fabled glare, Gorgons have other weapons available to them. They often possess tusks or fangs, as well as wings. There is a possible connection between the Gorgons' wings and the legend in which Perseus tore Medusa's head from her shoulders. If Gorgons can fly, they may have hollow bones—like birds. A weak skeleton could obviously be pulled apart more easily than a sturdy one. Hence their flight may be both a blessing and a curse. An especially adventurous hunter who enjoys the challenge of unarmed combat, or a person who is attacked by a Gorgon while unarmed, may be able to crush the monster's bones with a wrestling hold—while being careful, of course, to avoid eye contact. Once obtaining a grip on the creature, the hunter would be best served by closing his eyes and relying on his tactile sense instead.

Interestingly, a Gorgon's severed head is said to retain its power to turn people to stone. Hence a hunter who carefully decapitates a Gorgon and keeps its head will have acquired an extremely potent weapon. For obvious reasons, the head should be stored in an opaque container when not in use. One slight warning: there is ancient textual evidence that the drops of blood which fall from the decapitated head become snakes. These may be venomous, so a hunter should be careful that all the blood has dripped away before he carries the head as a weapon. However, if the snakes on a Gorgon's head are not poisonous, then this may also hold true for the snakes created by her blood. Moreover, the falling blood may only react with certain substances to produce the snakes. By letting the blood fall into a glass container rather than onto the ground, a hunter may be able to circumvent this transformation. If so, vials of a Gorgon's blood would provide another useful souvenir and weapon. They could be hurled at enemies, who would find themselves covered with snakes when the glass broke and the blood fell upon their bodies or the ground.

⚜ Summary ⚜

Dangers

- Petrifying gaze
- Snakes for hair
- Tusks or fangs
- Snakes formed from blood
- Wings

Weakness

- Weak bones (?)

Souvenirs

- Severed head
- Snake-generating blood

Selected Sources

Apollodorus. *Library* **2.4.2–3.** Description of Perseus's slaying of the Gorgon Medusa, and his subsequent use of her severed head to turn some of his enemies to stone. Apollodorus describes the Gorgons as having scales like dragons, tusks like boars, hands of bronze, and wings of gold.

Ovid. *Metamorphoses* **4.617–803.** An account of Medusa's slaying and various subsequent adventures Perseus had, including turning Atlas into a mountain. Ovid describes the Gorgon as having snakes on her head instead of hair. The poet claims that the blood that dripped from her severed head as Perseus flew over Libya fell to the ground and became the snakes that now infest that country.

⚜ Griffin ⚜

Description

*The griffin is a winged beast with the forequarters of an eagle
and the hindquarters of a lion. In size it resembles the dimensions
of a lion rather than an eagle. The monster is first mentioned in
ancient Greek texts, though these accounts suggest that the
creature is indigenous to Scythia rather than Greece itself—that is
to say, the region stretching from the Ukraine to central Asia.*

*Griffins are known to amass large quantities of gold, which
they dig out of the ground and store in their nests. Hence a
hunter who locates a griffin's horde will perhaps be able to
secure significant wealth. Naturally one may argue that the
pleasure of the hunt takes primacy over more sordid issues such
as money. Nevertheless, monster hunting can be an expensive
pursuit. Thus the acquisition of a griffin's gold may prove useful
in funding future hunts.*

*In addition to the gold, griffins are said to possess other rather
remarkable valuables that a hunter may obtain after a successful
hunt. According to medieval folklore, griffins' feathers can cure
blindness. The talons of a griffin are also of great interest, since
they will allegedly change color on contact with poison. Thus
they may be sold for a high price to those who fear assassination.*

Killing Methods

Though a truly magnificent creature, a blend of lion and eagle—
two most regal and splendid animals—the griffin is not difficult
to kill from a distance. A bow should prove sufficient to dispatch
the beast, as long as it comes within range. At close quarters,

however, a hunter should exercise extreme caution before engaging in combat with this particular monster. Griffins are savage and powerful, and their beaks, aquiline talons, and leonine claws are quite capable of tearing a man apart in a rather brutal fashion. Only the most fearless and skilled hunters should attempt to battle the creature with a sword, ax, or spear.

As with dragons, it is possible that a monster hunter could exploit the beast's attraction to gold by using that metal to lure it into a trap, or to bring it close to the ground if it persistently flies beyond the range of one's weapons. The drawback to this strategy is the potential cost involved, especially if the griffin manages to make off with the gold in question.

The griffin is perhaps not as impressive a foe as certain other beasts, and can be slaughtered in a simple and straightforward fashion. Thus they are considered to be a suitable prey for hunters of modest abilities. However, griffin hunts can prove exceptionally rewarding due to the aforementioned treasure they often possess, and the remarkable properties of their feathers and talons. Hence it is not unusual to find even the most experienced monster hunters tracking down griffins.

❦ Summary ❦

Dangers

- Beak
- Talons (front legs)
- Claws (rear legs)
- Flight

Weakness

- Attraction to gold

Souvenirs

- Handsome pelt
- Poison-detecting talons
- Blindness-curing feathers
- Gold

Selected Sources

Aelian. *De Natura Animalium* **4.27.** A detailed description of the beasts, and their habit of mining gold.

Crane, Thomas Frederick. *Italian Popular Tales.* **Boston: Houghton Mifflin, 1885, no. 8, 40–41.** A traditional Italian folktale in which a king asks his sons to acquire a griffin's feather to cure his blindness.

❧ Harpy ❧

Description

A Harpy is a winged hybrid of woman and bird, described in ancient Greek sources as inhabiting islands in the Mediterranean. They are of roughly human size and are armed with talons. There are variations within the species, as demonstrated in the ancient evidence, which depicts Harpies both with and without human arms. Similarly, they seem to vary in intelligence. Some are bestial, whereas others possess human speech—though both kinds are usually malicious. The monsters travel in packs, using numbers to compensate for their physical weakness.

Harpies are especially fond of ruining banquets, either stealing the food for their own use or befouling it to torment their human victims. They famously subjected the soothsayer Phineus to such treatment before being driven away by the Argonauts. Harpies also harassed Aeneas and his Trojans as they attempted to dine during their voyage to Italy.

Killing Methods

Harpies are one of the most insignificant kinds of monster. They have no weapons or powers of note, and can be slaughtered by a proficient archer, provided the hunter picks them off before they can fly away. The only potential dangers are their talons, and the possibility that those with human arms might be able to use weapons. However, there are no recorded instances of Harpies using tools, so this would be a rare occurrence indeed.

Slaughtering Harpies should be seen as little different from shooting pheasants, and unworthy of a serious hunting expedition.

However, they may provide useful target for first-time hunters. Also, given their habit of interfering with human dining, they should perhaps be killed on sight as a means of pest control.

·✤· Summary ·✤·

Dangers

- Flight
- Talons

Weakness

- Minimal strength

Selected Source

Apollodorus. *Library* **1.9.21.** A description of how the Harpies were driven away by the Argonauts.

ꙮ Hellhound ꙮ

Description

Hellhounds, as their name suggests, are infernal hounds. They have plagued human beings from ancient times onward, and are attested to in the writings of numerous cultures.

There are various different types of hellhound, though the most famous example is Cerberus. The great hero and legendary monster hunter Heracles was given the task of abducting this three-headed beast from the underworld as one of his twelve labors. Cerberus was a fearsome creature indeed. In addition to its three canine heads, the hound is described as having snake heads on its back, and a dragon's neck and head for a tail.

A different kind of hellhound is attested to in numerous British sources. The English hellhound is described as being a conventional hound in terms of shape, without the multiple heads or dragon tail of the Cerberus version of the monster. Yet it can easily be distinguished from a regular dog by the glowing, fiery red color of its eyes. While this form of hellhound may seem less fearsome, it may be more dangerous. Many sources describe it as being spectral, intangible. This would naturally present a major difficulty to any attempts to kill the creature.

Killing Methods

When examining how one might defeat a three-headed hellhound such as Cerberus, it is worth considering how that beast was defeated in combat by Heracles. According to the ancient sources, Heracles subdued Cerberus without weapons. He applied a powerful wrestling hold around one of the hound's three canine heads and forced it to yield. However, Heracles' strength may be somewhat beyond that of the average hunter, and grappling with a hellhound may prove more difficult than that incident might lead one to believe. In addition, Heracles was draped with an impenetrable lion's skin, which no doubt helped protect him from the creature's devastating jaws. Hence a modern hunter may wish to resort to weapons rather than unarmed combat, and perhaps neglect close combat altogether in favor of using ranged weapons. Such an approach would avoid the unpleasant risk of being leaped on and savaged by the hellhound.

The dragon's head bit Heracles, and hunters must be aware of its position at all times, lest it strike unexpectedly while the hunter is occupied with the primary heads. Also, the presence of this secondary head would make it difficult to stealthily approach such a hellhound from behind. As for the snake heads, they would prevent a hunter determined to grapple with the hound from leaping onto the creature's back in the hope of avoiding the bites of the three main heads.

Depending on its level of intelligence, it may be possible to disrupt a multiheaded hellhound by causing its heads to squabble. For example, a piece of meat could be thrown down in front of the creature, forcing each head to vie for it. Though the hellhound would have but a single stomach to satisfy, each head would presumably have its own taste buds, and therefore be eager to sample the meat. Obviously such a tactic would not be appropriate for a hunter attempting to slay the beast, as it would be completely unsporting, but it may be a viable method of escaping from such a creature if ambushed while unarmed.

The spectral or British type of hellhound, as alluded to above, may be a rather more challenging quarry. Clearly the destruction of an intangible creature raises some problems. However, there are sources that refer to such hellhounds savaging victims. If they can rend flesh, they must become tangible to do this. A hunter might therefore have to wait for the beast to become corporeal when it attacks, and slay it at close quarters as it pounces. He could alternatively lay out chunks of meat when stalking the beast, so it could be attacked after taking on material form to feed. This might again seem somewhat unsporting, though if the hunter merely used the meat to draw the hound out, and engaged it in combat rather than picking it off with an arrow as it ate, the tactic would be perfectly honorable.

An especially ambitious hunter may wish to capture rather than kill a hellhound. In much the same way that conventional hunters employ regular dogs, a monster hunter may be able to make good use of a trained hellhound. Such a creature could be used to flush out one's quarry, retrieve a target that has been shot down from the sky, or perhaps even help in open battle with a monster. Capturing a hellhound may not necessarily be as difficult as one would imagine. While Heracles used brute strength for this purpose, something perhaps beyond the capabilities of other men, one ancient source describes Cerberus being drugged. The prophetess known as the Sibyl, while leading the hero Aeneas through the underworld, threw down a honey cake laden with sedatives before the hound. Cerberus promptly devoured the cake and fell asleep. This would seem a sensible plan—far more effective than employing nets or snares against a creature that may have the power to become intangible. Ultimately, however, taming and training the captured hellhound may prove to be somewhat less easy, and hunters attempting this may wish to consult a skilled dog trainer for advice.

⚡ Summary ⚡

Dangers

- Teeth (possibly from multiple primary heads)
  - Secondary heads (e.g., on the tail)
    - Intangibility

Weaknesses

- Quarreling between heads (?)
  - Fondness for food

Souvenirs

- Pelt
- Man's best friend, or friends

Selected Sources

Apollodorus. *Library* **2.5.12.** A description of Cerberus, and Heracles' subduing of the creature.

Chambers, Robert. *The Book of Days*, **Vol. 2. Philadelphia: J. P. Lippincott, 1879, 433–36.** Accounts of various spectral hound sightings.

Virgil. *Aeneid* **6.17–23.** The drugging of Cerberus by the Sibyl.

⚜ Hydra ⚜

Description

A Hydra is a huge serpent with seven or nine heads, usually found dwelling in swamps and marshes. From the ancient evidence it appears that the monsters hunt alone, though with their many heads, battling a Hydra is akin to fighting a whole pack of enemies.

The true power of the Hydra lies in its ability to regenerate, and become more powerful after sustaining damage. When one of its heads is killed, two more will grow to replace it. Thus a hunter might suddenly find himself faced with dozens of snake heads biting at his flesh. It is unclear how many men fell to Hydras before the great Heracles discovered how to destroy the beasts and nullify their regenerative abilities. Even then, he found that one of the Hydra's heads was immortal—and hence had to be imprisoned rather than slain.

Hunters should be careful to avoid coming in contact with the creature's blood. According to legend this is a potent chemical that will bring an agonizing death to anyone who touches it. Heracles used it to poison his arrows. For those who wish to do likewise, be sure to store the blood in a cool, dark place, since apparently it is activated by heat (e.g., body heat). Such a virulent poison may prove useful on future hunts.

Killing Methods

The natural tendency when faced with so many snapping snake heads is a desire to start lopping them off. After all, decapitation is generally a pretty effective way to kill things. However, blindly following this instinct has sent many an unwary and unprepared

monster hunter to their grave, torn apart by the multitude of new heads that rose from the bloody necks of the old. One might assume that blunt weapons could avoid this, by crushing the beast's skulls rather than severing its necks and allowing the new heads to grow from the exposed stems. Yet according to Apollodorus's account, when Heracles used a club to kill the heads, two new heads still sprang up to replace each one he dispatched. Perhaps upon death a Hydra's head automatically falls off, freeing the neck stem so that the next ones can spawn.

Fortunately, this regenerative power can be overcome with fire. When Heracles' comrade Iolaus cauterized the neck stems after the death of each head, they no longer spawned new ones. A flaming torch or a supply of Greek fire might hence be excellent weapons to take on Hydra hunts. While sword or ax enthusiasts might like to decapitate each head prior to burning the necks, this is not absolutely necessary. As Heracles' use of his club indicates, one need only kill each head, not sever them from the body. A bow would probably suffice. If flaming arrows were used, then the weapon could perhaps do double duty—both killing each head and preventing regeneration.

As mentioned above, Heracles found that one of the Hydra's heads was immortal. If this proves to be accurate, then it would be advisable for a modern hunter to follow Heracles' lead and bury the head under a large rock. And then, of course, to move along quickly—perhaps posting warning signs to ensure that no one accidentally uncovers the beast.

❧ Summary ☙

Dangers

- Multiple heads, possibly with venomous bites
- Regenerative power, which will spawn additional heads
- Virulent chemical in its blood (for this reason, attempting to eat Hydra meat is not recommended)
- Possible immortality of one head

Weakness

- Fire

Souvenir

- Blood for poisoning one's weapons

Selected Sources

Apollodorus. *Library* **2.5.2.** Description of the Hydra, Heracles' battle with it, and how he killed it.

Pausanias. *Descriptions of Greece* **2.37.4.** Pausanias argues that the image of the Hydra's many heads was invented by the poet Peisander of Camirus, who wanted to spice up his verses. Pausanias suggests that in reality it was just a large water snake with a single head.

Sophocles. *Trachiniae* **749ff.** A description of Heracles' painful death after wearing a garment that had been treacherously anointed with Hydra's blood (or a centaur's blood that had been tainted with Hydra's blood, to be exact).

⊶ Kraken ⊷

Description

A kraken is a huge, tentacled sea monster resembling a giant octopus or squid. Specific mentions of the creature can be traced back to Renaissance Scandinavian sources, though there is no telling how many ships lost at sea in the ancient and medieval world were in reality destroyed by kraken attacks.

As with all creatures that spend the bulk of their time in the deepest parts of the ocean—beyond the reach and ken of mankind except when they rise to attack—information on krakens is limited. For example, we have no way of telling if the monsters live in packs with others of their kind, or individually. However, accounts of kraken attacks always involve a single member of the species— indicating that the latter is the case.

A kraken may be able to squirt ink, as do regular squids and octopi. While this substance is not poisonous (and can in fact be used as a tasty ingredient when cooking the creatures), it can obscure one's vision—allowing the monster to escape, or gain an advantage while attacking. Thus hunters should wear goggles that may be easily wiped clean.

There is an inherent danger in fighting a sea monster, since the hunters involved will have to leave the relative safety of land and entrust themselves to a more alien element. They will be atop the murky depths of the ocean, with only a ship between them and a watery grave. On land a hunter can flee if necessary. At sea, however, if one's craft is destroyed, there is nowhere to escape. Hence kraken hunters must be aware of the great risks they are undertaking.

Killing Methods

While a kraken can be killed by extreme physical damage, the size of the creature means that a large group of hunters armed with powerful ranged weapons would be required to destroy it. A kraken should not under any circumstances be attacked by a single hunter, nor should hunters attempt to engage a kraken in close-quarters combat. While the kraken's flesh can be parted by a decent blade, in the event of a battle the hunters will likely be kept at bay by the beast's tentacles. While they are hacking away at these, the kraken may be destroying their ship. The advantage of numerous arms is the ability to multitask in such a fashion. Hence harpoons and other ranged weapons are essential when hunting a kraken, so that the creature's head can be targeted from a distance.

Though the use of fire against a creature swimming in the ocean may at first seem dubious, it is possible. Of course, conventional flames will be extinguished by the sea, but throughout history there have been chemical weapons designed to burn heavily even on contact with water. Greek fire is perhaps the most famous example. A team of hunters could coat an area of the ocean with such a substance, which would then be set ablaze during the battle with the kraken.

Given the creature's similarities to the squid and the octopus, a kraken may have a similar taste. Therefore hunters can potentially look forward to a good meal following a successful kraken hunt.

❧ Summary ☙

Dangers

- Immense size and power
  - Ink

Weakness

- Soft, easily wounded flesh

Souvenirs

- Vast amounts of calamari

Selected Source

Pontoppidan, Erich. *The Natural History of Norway*, Vol. 2. London: A. Linde, 1755, 210–8. An early account of kraken sightings.

Manticore

Description

A manticore is a beast with the head of a man, the body of a red lion, and the tail of a scorpion. It is of approximately leonine size, and armed with the flesh-rending claws of a large feline.

The creature is extremely swift, and has three layers of razor-sharp teeth in its mouth, promising to maim, mutilate, and eviscerate any who stray too near to the beast. It also can kill with its barbed scorpion's tail, the venom of which threatens to bring an agonizing death to its victims. According to the ancient Greek writer Pausanias, the manticore can even hurl barbs from this tail at distant victims. The monster is said to be especially fond of human flesh, and will thus readily use these fearsome weapons against any person it encounters.

Despite the appearance of its head, which is described as resembling that of a man but for its three rows of teeth, it does not seem that the manticore has human intelligence. There is no indication in the ancient source material that it can speak, and the Roman writer Pliny the Elder declares that it makes a sound like the mixture of a flute and a trumpet, rather than possessing human speech.

Pliny lists the manticore among the beasts of Ethiopia, whereas Pausanias connects them with India. Therefore it is possible that they are indigenous to both regions.

Killing Methods

Engaging in close combat with a manticore should be avoided by all but the most highly skilled. Even with a normal lion, its powerful body, deadly claws, and savage teeth would make it a formidable foe at close quarters. The manticore has yet another weapon in its poisonous tail with which to overwhelm a human attacker. Thus hunters may wish to employ bows on manticore hunts, and bring the monster down from a distance. Even so, they must be careful to avoid barbs launched from the creature's tail, and might consider carrying shields to defend against them.

If a hunter is determined to battle a manticore at close quarters, he would also be well advised to use a shield in addition to his sword, ax, spear, or club. This would enable him to fend off the creature's claws, teeth, and tail. He also may wish to lop off the manticore's tail during the first exchange of blows, since that is perhaps the monster's most dangerous weapon. With the tail removed, the manticore will have lost its weapon of greatest reach, and be forced to fight like any other large cat. Still a fearsome opponent, no doubt, but far easier to fend off and strike.

A note of warning: while it is common for lion hunters to decapitate a beast and have its head mounted for a trophy, this is under no circumstances to be done with a manticore. Since the creature bears the head of a man, having such an object mounted in one's home may bring about legal difficulties—not to mention nightmares for any children inhabiting the home. Therefore it is recommended that hunters instead retain the beast's blood-red pelt or scorpion's tail if a souvenir is desired.

❧ Summary ❧

Dangers

- Teeth
- Claws
- Poisonous tail

Weakness

- Its bright red fur provides terrible camouflage in most environments, making it easy to spot

Souvenirs

- Splendid red pelt
- Tail

Selected Sources

Pliny the Elder. *Natural History* **8.30.** A description of the manticore among other creatures that Pliny attributes to Ethiopia.

Pausanias. *Descriptions of Greece* **9.21.4–5.** Another description of the manticore, though in this case Pausanias considers the beast to be a fictional exaggeration of the tiger.

~~⚜~~ Merman ~~⚜~~

Description

Mermen, or Tritones, as they are called in ancient Hellenic sources, are creatures with the upper body of a human and the lower body of a fish. They possess human intelligence and are often described as wielding weapons—primarily tridents. Mermen can commonly be encountered both alone or in groups.

Though in children's stories mermen tend to be portrayed as innocent, benign creatures, there are many accounts in ancient literature and folklore of their malicious acts against human beings. According to Pausanias, a Triton dwelling off the coast of Tanagra in Greece would prey on women when they came to wash in the sea prior to taking part in the rites of the god Dionysus. He would also steal cattle and even attack small boats. His crimes were brought to an end only when he was slain by Dionysus himself, or drugged with wine and decapitated by a man of Tanagra, depending on which account one believes.

Killing Methods

The major difficultly with hunting mermen is that, unlike the larger oceanic monsters, they generally do not to rise and attack ships. Instead they prey on lone, vulnerable humans who stray close to the water. This means that they must be sought out. While an extremely fortunate individual may catch a merman sunning itself on a rock, and be able to pick the creature off with an arrow, such occurrences will be rare. The Triton that assaulted the people of Tanagra was apparently lured to his doom by the smell of wine, and killed when he drank it and fell into a stupor.

Hence it is possible that some of the creatures can be drawn onto the shore. However, such kills are considered to be less than sporting—akin to shooting fish in a barrel. A true hunter will usually entrust himself to the water if he wishes to track down these half-piscine beings, and slay them in a respectable fashion.

Under the waves a hunter is limited in his choice of weapons, and inhibited by his inferior mobility. Needless to say, attempting to swing an ax or a sword underwater would be a rather pointless activity—especially when battling a creature that is designed for such an environment and can dart around with perfect agility. Moreover, the hunter would rely on breathing apparatus for his survival. Were a merman to damage this in combat, the hunter would be forced to experience the rather unpleasant death granted to those who drown.

If the depictions of Tritones in ancient Greek art provide accurate insights into the mermen, they may be tool-using creatures armed with spears or tridents. Hence they would be dangerous opponents in a submarine battle. It is therefore recommended that hunters employ ranged weapons such as harpoon guns rather than attempting to duel with mermen at close quarters.

✺ Summary ✺

Dangers

- Underwater advantages
- Spears and tridents (?)

Weaknesses

- Helpless on land
- Possible attraction to wine

Selected Sources

Pausanias. *Descriptions of Greece* 9.20.4–5. A description of how a Triton attacked people near Tanagra until it was slain.

Pontoppidan, Erich. *The Natural History of Norway*, Vol. 2. London: A. Linde, 1755, 186–95. An account of various merman sightings.

~~⚬~~ Minotaur ~~⚬~~

Description

A Minotaur possesses the body of a man but the head of a bull. The monster was named after the most famous example of the species— the Minotaur of Crete, in turn named after King Minos. This particular Minotaur was created following a tryst between Minos's queen and a magical bull. Minos had an elaborate labyrinth created to house the monster, into which he sent captive Athenians to be devoured by the beast. However, the eponymous Minotaur's reign of terror was ended when the hero Theseus entered the labyrinth and slew the beast.

Killing Methods

Minotaurs can in theory be killed by any weapon, since their human body and bovine head share all the weaknesses and vulnerabilities of the respective species they resemble. Swords, axes, clubs, and arrows can pierce their flesh or break their bones (though bulls have rather thick skulls, and the monster's cranium will hence be somewhat resistant to damage). However, the savage ferocity of the creature means that it would be inadvisable for physically weak hunters to attempt to engage one in hand-to-hand combat, as this would probably result in a severe goring.

Physically powerful hunters, on the other hand, may enjoy the challenge of entering into unarmed combat with a Minotaur. The Greek hero Theseus can be seen wrestling with the beast in various ancient artworks, and this feat of strength, skill, and courage earned him great renown. Of course, there is a fine history of mighty hunters such as Heracles using wrestling techniques against monsters. An ambitious modern hunter may wish to follow in this tradition.

If wrestling with a Minotaur, one might be well advised to attack the creature's neck. A bull's head weighs significantly more than a man's head, meaning that the monster's human neck could be under greater stress than it was ideally designed for. In addition, the horns would provide excellent leverage for a hunter who wished to apply pressure to a Minotaur's neck, in the hope of breaking it.

❧ Summary ❧

Dangers

- Horns
- Aggressive

Weakness

- Weak neck (?)

Selected Sources

Apollodorus. *Epitome* **1.9.** Theseus is described as punching the Minotaur to death.

Plutarch. *Life of Theseus* **19.2–3.** Plutarch relates an alternative tale in which Theseus merely wrestled and defeated a Cretan general named Taurus. Alas, such base skepticism has long surrounded the fine art of monster hunting.

Mummy

Description

Mummies were originally human corpses, embalmed and wrapped in bandages as part of an ancient Egyptian ritual designed to preserve bodies prior to entombment. However, through dark magic—for example, curses designed to bring about the destruction of grave robbers—they have arisen as undead creatures.
Mummies are shambling, slow-moving creatures. Even so, they can be deadly if they are able to seize hold of a victim. According to ancient inscriptions, mummies are fond of seizing their victims by the neck, and no doubt possess supernatural strength with which to crush throats or perhaps even break necks.

Killing Methods

The process of ancient Egyptian mummification involved removing many of the organs from the body. From the Eighteenth Dynasty onward, this included the brain. Therefore hunters should not expect to slay a mummy by piercing its skull. While some organs, most notably the heart, were not removed, a hunter should not assume that destroying these will destroy the mummy. The creatures are animated by the power of a curse, and do not require their ancient, withered organs in order to function.

Hence a hunter should completely destroy a mummy's body if he wishes to terminate the monster. Fire would be useful for this purpose. A mummy's dry bandages would be ideal fuel, making incineration both easy and practical. Alternatively, an adventurous hunter may wish to hack a mummy to pieces with a sword or an

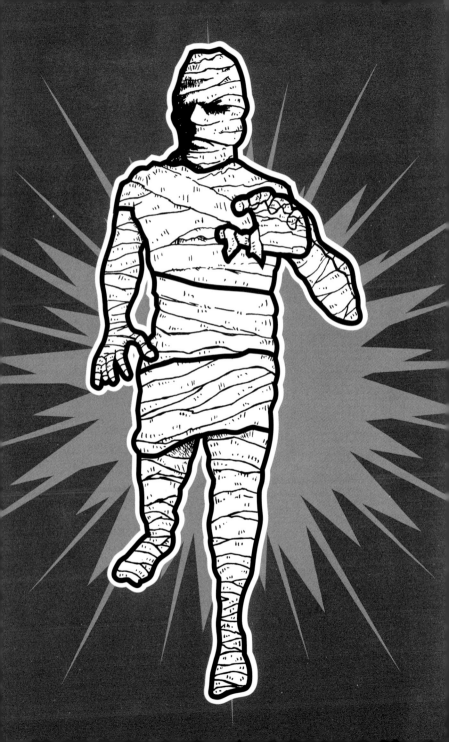

ax. However, a hunter engaging in close combat with a mummy should be careful to avoid being strangled.

If a hunter unexpectedly encounters a mummy and has no suitable weapons on hand with which to destroy it, he should simply walk away at a brisk pace. Mummies are notoriously slow-moving creatures, so it should be but a simple matter to escape from the scene and return when one has a weapon. Since most mummies reside in museums, there should be numerous items of weaponry available on the premises that may be employed if a mummy's curse is activated and it becomes animated.

Though it may be tempting to set fire to every Egyptian exhibition one comes across to preemptively immolate any mummies before they pose a threat, such a course of action would be inadvisable. In addition to being totally unsporting, it would be badly received by museum staff.

Summary

Danger

- Strangulation

Weaknesses

- Fire
- Slow, lumbering pace

Selected Sources

Lichtheim, Miriam. *Ancient Egyptian Literature*, Vol. 1, *The Old and Middle Kingdoms*. Berkeley: University of California Press, 1975, 24. An inscription in which the occupant of a tomb threatens to seize intruders by the neck.

Smith, G. Elliot, and William R. Dawson. *Egyptian Mummies*. London: G. Allen & Unwin, 1924. A detailed analysis of ancient Egyptian mummification.

Pegasus

Description

The Pegasus is a winged horse. They are usually considered to be of ancient Greek origin, though Pliny the Elder suggests that they are indigenous to Ethiopia. These creatures were often used as mounts by Hellenic monster hunters. Bellerophon flew on the back of a Pegasus when he killed the Chimera, and according to some accounts Perseus rode one when fleeing the immortal Gorgons who pursued him after the slaying of Medusa.

Capturing Methods

Should one wish to kill a Pegasus, the task would be easy enough. It would be no more difficult than bringing down a horse, as long as it was not given the opportunity to fly out of range. However, no serious monster hunter would condone such an act. To the monster-hunting community Pegasi are noble steeds, and of tremendous use on hunts. Thus the creature is included in this work only to bring it to the attention of those new to the field of cryptozoology, and for the benefit of aspiring monster hunters who may wish to capture one.

It takes little imagination to appreciate how useful a winged steed would be when hunting down flying monsters, which might otherwise be able to stay beyond a hunter's reach. It would also be possible with such a mount to fly above the reach of powerful nonflying monsters, and attack them from a safe distance. This is what Bellerophon did when battling the Chimera. He took to the skies atop a Pegasus, and slaughtered it from the air.

It is recommended that hunters ambush a Pegasus with

weighted nets to prevent it from escaping, and proceed to tame it. Pegasi are not known to be violent or temperamental creatures, and are easily broken in. Hunters unfamiliar with horses would be well served to employ or at least seek advice from a skilled trainer of such animals before attempting to tame and train a Pegasus.

Summary

Danger

- Flight

Weakness

- Calm temperament

Souvenir

- The creature itself

Selected Sources

Apollodorus. *Library* 2.3.2. An account of Bellerophon shooting down the Chimera while riding a Pegasus.

Pliny the Elder. *Natural History* 8.30. Pliny claims that Pegasi are indigenous to Ethiopia and that they bear horns in addition to wings.

⋰⋱ Roc ⋰⋱

Description

A roc is a huge bird. The creature is usually encountered at sea, since it dwells on isolated islands. Different sources tend to place its domains as close to Madagascar or Arabia.

Rocs can be extremely aggressive, and are capable of using weapons of sorts in addition to their fearsome beaks and talons. There are tales of rocs lifting huge boulders and dropping them from a great height to smash the ships of their victims.

Should a hunter succeed in dispatching one or more of these creatures, he would naturally obtain a large supply of avian meat. This could provide a party of hunters with a useful source of low-fat sustenance to be either consumed or sold to local culinary establishments. The same would be true of the roc's eggs, if recovered.

Killing Methods

Given the monster's huge size, a roc (or *rukh*, as it is often spelled) could hardly be picked out of the sky with a casual volley of spears or arrows. It would require an extremely accurate shot to a critical location to bring down such a creature. Hunters should be prepared for a long, drawn-out fight requiring numerous such projectiles—unless poison is used to enhance their lethality. Engaging a roc with close-combat weapons would be foolhardy and all but impossible.

Battling a roc is, of course, a rather dangerous affair, making it somewhat unique in the realm of fowling. While hunters who bring down birds usually do so from a position of complete safety, this is certainly not true when hunting rocs. There are accounts of these birds carrying off creatures as large as elephants, dropping them to their deaths from a great height, and feasting on their smashed carcasses. Hence they would find little difficulty in devouring unfortunate human beings.

Hunters must also be aware that rocs can return fire, so to speak, by attempting to drop boulders on them. Therefore it would be advisable to remain highly mobile when hunting rocs, so that one could take evasive action in the event of boulders being thrown, instead of presenting a stationary and thus highly vulnerable target. However, the roc's choice of armaments, potentially devastating though they might be, would possibly work in a hunter's favor. When carrying large boulders, the birds would presumably be slower in flight and hence easier to shoot down.

❧ Summary ❧

Dangers

- Immense size
  - Beak
  - Talons
  - Boulders

Weakness

- An easy target due to its size

Souvenirs

- Vast supplies of white meat
  - Huge eggs

Selected Sources

Burton, Richard, trans. *The Arabian Nights: Tales from a Thousand and One Nights.* **New York: Modern Library, 2001, 367.** A description of two rocs attacking a ship with boulders.

Marco Polo. *The Travels of Marco Polo.* **London: Penguin, 1958, 300–1.** An account of what the author was told about rocs during his travels in and around Madagascar. Marco Polo connected these creatures with griffins, though he acknowledged that the local inhabitants described them as being huge birds rather than a mixture of eagle and lion.

⁕ Sasquatch ⁕

Description

A Sasquatch is an apelike creature, most commonly sited in North America and the Himalayas. Accounts and evidence indicate that some breeds of Sasquatch are of roughly human size, though others might be somewhat larger.

The Sasquatch, also commonly known as Bigfoot or the yeti (the latter usually with regard to the Himalayan breed), is something of a celebrity in the monster world. It is arguably the most sought out and contemplated by hunters and cryptozoologists. However, it is also a rather elusive and mysterious creature.

There are no records of hunters killing a Sasquatch—demonstrating just how hardy, cunning, and stealthy they must be. Any monster hunter who managed to track down and kill a Sasquatch would earn a great deal of prestige among his peers.

Killing Methods

The Sasquatch most likely possesses great strength, perhaps equivalent to that of a large gorilla. Hence hunters may wish to avoid close combat with these creatures, since their power and ferocity would make them formidable opponents. From a distance, on the other hand, a hunter has a considerably better chance. Should its bones be especially dense, however, an arrow would likely not prove sufficient unless it struck a critical area of soft tissue such as the throat, so precision is in order. Hunters should always be prepared to deliver more than one shot, should the first fail to bring down the target.

There is one additional factor to consider when hunting a

Sasquatch. There have been various instances of these creatures being filmed or photographed. Yet in each case the resulting images tend to be blurred. If this phenomenon was the case on only a handful of occasions, one might be tempted to blame the skill of the cameramen or the quality of their equipment. But since it is so universal, other possibilities must be considered. The Sasquatch may be able to distort the space directly around it, causing it to become slightly out of synch with the rest of the world and therefore impossible to perceive clearly. Such a super-natural ability may have been developed as a means of confusing and thus repelling attackers. Hunters must, of course, be prepared to take this into account. Depending on how blurred an area becomes, it may be difficult for a hunter to take aim without becoming disorientated. It would be advisable for hunters to train for such an occurrence, and become accustomed to firing at an out-of-focus target. A hunter who wears spectacles may wish to remove these prior to practicing his shooting. A hunter with good eyesight could wear powerful glasses to achieve the same effect. Alternatively, he could become intoxicated—though hunters should exercise caution when operating weapons after the heavy consumption of alcohol.

❧ Summary ❧

Dangers

- Physical strength
- Ability to distort space (?)

Weakness

- Despite their seeming elusiveness, they are more frequently caught on film than other monsters. This perhaps indicates that they are occasionally overconfident in their abilities to escape from danger and are willing to stray near humans.

Souvenir

- The pelt or stuffed body of a Sasquatch would earn a hunter everlasting fame.

Selected Source

Green, John. *On the Track of the Sasquatch*. Blaine, Wash.: Hancock House, 1995. A discussion of the creature and various notable sightings.

❧ Scorpion Man ❧

Description

A scorpion man is a monster similar to a centaur, in that it possesses the upper body of a man attached to the body of an animal. However, in this case, an oversized scorpion provides the lower half. The scorpion man is first described and depicted in ancient Mesopotamian sources. It is difficult to ascertain exactly what size the creatures are, but in one notable surviving artwork they appear to be of approximately human dimensions.

Scorpion men are worthy adversaries, combining the dangers of both a human opponent and a beast. They are intelligent beings, capable of speech, of using weapons in their human hands, and of fighting in an organized group. At the same time, they possess the deadly barbed tail of the scorpion, which would no doubt inflict a painful death on any hunter who had the misfortune to be transfixed by it. It is worth remembering that even the great hero Gilgamesh trembled in fear upon encountering these monsters. His fear abated only when the scorpion men decided not to devour him on account of his semidivine status. Naturally the average hunter would not be able to rely on the same courtesy.

Killing Methods

In close combat, hunters would be forced to deal with any weapons the scorpion man might be holding, as well as its lethal tail. This could be problematic, especially if these monsters are skilled in the use of arms—meaning that they could hold the hunter's weapons at bay while creating an opening for a fatal tail strike. In addition, it is unclear whether scorpion men have pincers as part of their lower body. If so, these would present two additional extremely dangerous threats. Hence hunters may wish to avoid single combat at close quarters, and only engage scorpion men in melee if they have the advantage of numbers. Three hunters in tandem would probably be necessary to deal with a scorpion man with pincers. Should they in fact not possess such appendages, on the other hand, then a single skilled hunter should suffice. If a hunter does choose to fight at close range with a scorpion man, he might consider destroying one or more of the beast's legs to limit its mobility. While a regular scorpion may be able to function well even after losing a leg, a scorpion man's lower body has to support the additional weight of the human torso. Hence even the destruction of one limb might render the monster immobile.

Slaying a scorpion man from a distance would no doubt be easier. However, as tool-using creatures they would be able to return fire with spears or bows. Therefore caution should still be exercised.

❧ Summary ❧

Dangers

- Intelligent, tool-using creature
- Scorpion's tail
- Pincers (?)

Weakness

- Destroying one of its front legs may render it unable to support its human torso

Selected Sources

Enuma Elish **1.121–24.** Scorpion men are listed as being among the goddess Tiamat's vast host of monsters, and described as bearing weapons.

The Epic of Gilgamesh, **tablet 9.** A description of Gilgamesh's encounter with the scorpion men.

~✵. Siren .✵~

Description

A Siren possesses the upper body of a woman attached to the lower body of a bird. They are of approximately human size, and can usually be found dwelling in groups on isolated islands—especially those between Greece and Turkey, according to the ancient sources.

Sirens prey upon the crews of ships that draw close to their island, beguiling them and luring them to their doom with their enchanted singing. The Sirens' song offers hidden knowledge to those who hear it. They claim to know everything that occurs in the world, and entice their victims with all that they could reveal—bewitching them with the power of their music until the fools truly believe they will obtain what they desire if they only submit.

Killing Methods

Of all the monsters in the world, Sirens perhaps require the least effort to kill. If a potential victim can resist the magical lure of their song then these bizarre songstresses will take their own lives.

Should a hunter wish to take a more active part in their deaths, any weapon should suffice. Sirens are not known to possess any special protections or resistances. Any ranged weapon, such as a bow or a sling, or melee weapon, such as a sword or a mace, will serve the purpose admirably.

Despite these vulnerabilities, however, a Siren can still provide a serious danger to unprepared hunters. Their harmonies are so beguiling that even Odysseus, one of the most cunning and determined heroes of all time, had to be lashed to the mast of his ship so he would not leap into the ocean and swim to his doom. Fortunately the song has to be heard for it to have an effect. Thus blocking one's ears will nullify it. During the voyage of the Argonauts, the legendary bard Orpheus is said to have used his own music to drown out that of the Sirens. In the absence of earplugs, a hunter who encounters Sirens might be able to survive by breaking into song while he escapes from or dispatches them.

It is unknown whether the song has any effect on animals. It seems unlikely since it offers knowledge to the listeners—something that is likely to appeal specifically to humans rather than beasts. Hence those with a preference for hunting with hounds could perhaps employ them against this particular monster.

Summary

Danger

- Bewitching song

Weakness

- Suicidal tendencies

Selected Sources

Apollodorus. *Epitome* **7.19.** An account of how the Sirens perished after Odysseus and his men escaped.

Apollonius of Rhodes. *Argonautica* **4.885–921.** The Argonauts' encounter with the Sirens, during which Orpheus countered their music with his own.

Homer. *Odyssey* **12.158–200.** Odysseus's encounter with the creatures. He remained tied to the mast while his crew, their ears blocked with wax, sailed the ship past the Sirens' island.

~❧ Sphinx ❧~

Description

*The Sphinx is a winged creature with the head of a woman
attached to the body of a lion. The Sphinx appears in both
ancient Egyptian artworks, most notably the famous sculpture of
the monster at Giza, and in ancient Greece sources. On Hellenic
vases the Sphinx is of slightly smaller than human size, perhaps
indicating that the huge Egyptian sculptures are larger-than-life
renditions of the beast. However, given the nature of ancient
Greek vase painting, it is equally possible that the artists
downplayed the creature's size somewhat for aesthetic reasons.
Sphinxes are intelligent creatures, capable of speech. In fact, they
take great pleasure in posing riddles to passersby, and slaying those
who fail to answer them correctly. However, answering the riddle
correctly will bring about the beast's destruction. When Oedipus did
so, the Sphinx that had been plaguing the ancient Greek city of
Thebes committed suicide.*

Killing Methods

Given that a single Sphinx was able to terrorize Thebes, it must
be assumed that these creatures are highly resistant to blades,
clubs, and bows. Were this not the case, then the Theban warriors
would surely have destroyed the monster plaguing their
settlement. Instead the beast was slain only when Oedipus
answered its riddle, and it subsequently flung itself to its death.

The death of the Theban Sphinx illustrates a rather important
point that hunters should note well. While Sphinxes may be

highly resistant to physical damage, their suicidal tendencies are powerful and relatively easy to exploit. When a potential victim proves their equal, and answers their riddles correctly, the Sphinxes are distraught at their lack of mental dominance, and take their own lives in a fit of rage and shame.

While it is likely that each Sphinx will utilize its own favorite riddle, it is worth remembering the specific riddle employed by the Theban Sphinx in case a hunter encounters another Sphinx that uses it. The riddle is as follows: "What walks on four legs in the morning, two legs in the afternoon, three legs in the evening, and is weakest when it has most?" The answer is man, and the riddle refers respectively to a crawling babe, a full-grown man, and an aged man who walks with a cane.

Given the psychological profile one may construct of these creatures from the Theban episode, it is possible that a Sphinx may also be driven to despair and suicide if challenged with a riddle it cannot answer. Such an event would likewise reveal the hunter's mental superiority and hopefully bring about the monster's death.

Summary

Danger

- Claws

Weakness

- Suicidal tendencies

Selected Source

Apollodorus. *Library* **3.5.8.** An account of the Theban Sphinx, its riddle, and its death.

~~⚜~~ Troll ~~⚜~~

Description

Trolls are grotesque humanoid creatures, sometimes with multiple heads upon their hideous bodies. They have a taste for human flesh and thus prey upon any person unfortunate enough to enter the forests or marshes in which they dwell. The creatures appear to be of Scandinavian origin, and are widely attested to in medieval sources from that region.

Trolls are strong creatures, capable of tearing weak men apart. In Norse literature, it was mighty Thor who was famous for slaughtering these monsters—indicating that they were considered to be suitable opponents for even the greatest of gods and heroes.

However, though they are dangerous adversaries, trolls can often be overcome via human cunning. While trolls use tools and can speak, rather than being mindless beasts, they do tend to be rather stupid creatures. A prime illustration of this would be the story of a man called Boots. He was captured by trolls who intended to devour him. However, shortly before he was due to be killed, he offered to sharpen the knife with which he was to be slaughtered. One of the trolls allowed him to do so. Once the knife was sharp, Boots suggested that he test the blade on the troll's hair, to ensure that the edge was sharp enough. Again the idiotic troll agreed, and placed her head near him. Boots promptly decapitated her and made good his escape. As this tale demonstrates, deception and trickery are definitely viable strategies against trolls.

Killing Methods

Considering the trolls' history of battling with gods such as Thor, a hunter may wish to think twice before engaging a troll at close quarters. While it is by no means impossible to hack these monsters to pieces with a sword or an ax, only hunters who are assured of their strength and skill should attempt this.

As alluded to above, particularly powerful trolls often have multiple heads. In some cases individual trolls are recorded as having six or even nine heads. This abundance of brains, eyes, and ears may make it difficult to stalk a troll and approach it undetected. It would also prevent a hunter from eliminating a troll with a single toss of a spear or thrust of a blade to the brain—since the remaining heads would continue to function. Logically one might wish to simply target the body of a multiheaded troll instead, and destroy its heart or another vital organ. However, there is evidence that such trolls can regenerate their injured parts, including ruined heads. Therefore they can be destroyed only if all the heads are killed in rapid succession. This could prove very difficult in a close-quarters combat situation, since a hunter would have to penetrate the troll's defenses several times within what would perhaps be a very small window of opportunity. Should he fail to do so, and his subsequent attacks be blocked or parried by the troll, then the previously smashed or cloven heads would be able to reconstruct themselves.

To overcome a many-headed troll's regenerative abilities, a hunter could attempt to launch a series of ranged attacks in quick succession, in the hope of beating the troll's rate of reconstruction. A volley of well-placed arrows might be effective, slaying all the heads before the first can come back to life. Alternatively, incendiary weapons such as flaming torches, fire-tipped arrows, or Greek fire could be used to immolate the creature. Even if the flames did not consume all the heads at once, they might prevent the damaged heads from regenerating. Such is the case with the Hydra, and it may also hold true for trolls.

~✤ Summary ✤~

Dangers

- Great strength
- Regeneration

Weakness

- Low intelligence

Selected Sources

Sturlson, Snorri. *The Prose Edda: Gylfaginning* 42. Refers to Thor journeying into lands inhabited by trolls so that he might slay them.

Dasent, George Webbe. *Popular Tales from the Norse.* New York: G. P. Putnam's Sons, 1904, 215–21. An account of how Boots robbed a troll, was captured, and used his cunning to escape; **357–69.** An account of how a princess's companion—a magical bull—battled a series of multiheaded trolls.

⋙ Vampire ⋙

Description

A vampire is an undead creature that rises from its grave to feed on the blood of the living. The vampire is of uncertain origin and can be found in the chronicles of numerous cultures around the world. Since this work is designed to cover numerous monsters, it cannot devote the vast space that would be needed to chronicle all the different forms of vampire that exist around the world. Therefore it will focus on the European form of the creature, since this is the most common.

Vampires are dangerous adversaries, and should therefore be treated with the utmost caution. Their inhuman strength and speed, combined with their rather uncultured refusal to die from most injuries, make them potentially difficult to terminate. In addition, their ability to spread their contagion when they kill means that careless hunters could themselves become vampires— and therefore a danger to their fellows. While vampire lore is inconsistent as to whether vampirism is spread to a victim through the vampire's bite, or merely to any individual slain by a vampire, the fact remains that this is a serious concern.

Though some vampires are little more than savage beasts, others are extremely intelligent. Not only can they match wits with their prey, and fight or hunt with great cunning, but some can even masquerade as human beings and live seemingly innocent lives within the societies they victimize.

Those vampires who do not thus dwell in villages or cities can be found in a variety of abodes when not out feeding—ranging from the graves in which they were buried to lavish castles in the case of aristocratic vampires.

Though their humanlike appearance may seem far removed from the fearsome spectacle of a dragon or Hydra, vampires are considered to be among the most challenging of all quarries. Hence slaying vampires can attract a great deal of prestige in the monster-hunting community, especially if the vampires in question are particularly powerful creatures that have walked the earth and fed on victims for centuries. Vampires are especially good targets for hunters who prefer urban environments and lack the inclination or the ability to spend large amounts of time trekking through swamps and forests, or visiting isolated islands and mountain ranges in search of their prey.

Killing Methods

Vampires are strong, fast, and cunning foes. Fortunately, however, their considerable powers are balanced by several notable vulnerabilities. A vampire will die when its heart is pierced by a wooden object, for example. Hence bows and crossbows would be ideal, though of course one must make sure to use wooden arrows or quarrels rather than metal missiles. The traditional stake through the heart would also be a suitable method of delivering destruction to a vampire, though if attempted on a mobile vampire this could prove difficult, depending on that particular creature's strength, speed, and fighting skills. A stake could be thrust into the heart of a sleeping vampire, though naturally this would be rather unsporting—and earn one little acclaim among fellow monster hunters. Hunters who are determined to engage with a vampire at melee range may wish to use spears rather than stakes for the increased range and combat effectiveness. Mounting wooden tips on swords may also be possible.

Numerous sources state that a vampire may be returned to the embrace of true, honest death by decapitation. This may be another point in favor of using a sword with a wooden tip, since such a weapon would provide two possible avenues by which it could deliver destruction. However, some sources specify a sexton's shovel to be the necessary weapon in the decapitation of a vampire. Even if one were to find a sexton, or church employee, willing to loan his spade to a hunter, such a tool would not naturally lend itself to mortal combat. It would be somewhat difficult to fight a mobile vampire with a shovel.

According to certain pieces of evidence, silver can harm vampires. Some of these go so far as to say that a silver dagger can be used in place of a wooden stake to transfix a vampire's heart. Swords or axes of silver could possibly also be used to slay these creatures, though the production of such objects could be expensive. Silver-tipped arrows would perhaps be a less costly alternative, since less of the metal would have to be used.

A method of dealing with vampires that can be found in much of the source material is fire. Incineration can destroy these monsters, which should surely be of delight to part-time pyromaniacs. Yet a note of caution should be raised. Given their supernatural speed, a burning vampire might be able to suddenly leap upon a hunter. This is clearly undesirable. Hence a hunter must not be overconfident, and should attempt to bring about incineration as rapidly as possible.

It seems well established that vampires may be harmed by sacred objects such as a crucifix, a communion wafer, or holy water. Thus a hunter may wish to raid his local place of worship before engaging vampires, and acquire as many such items as possible. A hunter might also consider having his weapons blessed by a priest, in case this would increase their ability to inflict damage against the undead.

Vampires allegedly have an aversion to garlic. While garlic is hardly the most suitable of weapons, it could be carried to ward off vampires. A hunter favoring ranged combat may wish to use garlic to fend off a vampire that has drawn too close, for example.

Hunters should be warned that according to certain tales, vampires can become intangible, allowing them to leave their graves or crypts without breaking them open or clawing their way out of the earth. It goes without saying that killing an intangible creature would be problematic. However, it is said that vampires cannot become intangible shortly after drinking blood. Hence a hunter who has located the area in which a vampire hunts or dwells may wish to place a bowl filled with fresh blood in a suitable position, in the hope that the monster will be unable to resist the allure of the crimson liquid, and become anchored to the material world.

⤙❧ Summary ☙⤚

Dangers

- Supernatural strength and speed
- Cursed bite
- Possible ability to become intangible

Weaknesses

- Fire
- Holy objects
- Wood (if it pierces the heart)
- Silver
- Garlic

Selected Sources

MacDougall, Shane. *The Vampire Slayers' Field Guide to the Undead*. Doylestown, Pa.: Strider Nolan, 2003. This work, though it often descends into childish frivolity and includes a discussion of fiction along with information about real monsters, provides a useful guide to the many creatures around the world that commonly fall under the term *vampire*. Since many of these have powers and weaknesses different from those described above, a serious vampire hunter would be well advised to research them.

Summers, Montague. *The Vampire*. London: Senate, 1995; *The Vampire in Europe: True Tales of the Undead*. New York: Gramercy, 1996. These two volumes provide a detailed discussion of vampire lore, and numerous case studies.

Wright, Dudley. *The Book of Vampires*. Detroit: Omni-graphics, 1999. A chronicle of vampire encounters from various times and places.

❧ Wendigo ☙

Description

A wendigo is a large, ghostly beast that feasts on human flesh. The creature is of North American origin, and since Native American tribes did not possess a literary tradition until settlers from Europe arrived in the Western Hemisphere, information on wendigos was preserved in their oral history. Therefore it is impossible to be precisely certain which versions of wendigo lore are the most ancient or the most reliable. Hunters must hence be wary, and prepared for any wendigo they face to manifest powers and abilities from any of the many divergent tales concerning these monsters.

Wendigos are often described as being large, fur-covered beasts with savage teeth. They are said to be fast, powerful, and capable of stealthily tracking their prey through forests. Even the most skilled of hunters would have to be careful to avoid being ambushed by a wendigo. In addition to these dangerous physical attributes, wendigo are reputed to be able to become intangible phantoms—making it even easier for them to creep up to their victims undetected, their spectral bodies making no sound against the ground.

Killing Methods

Wendigos are supposedly resistant to most forms of physical harm. Yet they can be slain by fire, making flaming torches, fire-tipped arrows, or Greek fire valuable tools when hunting the creatures. In addition, they are vulnerable to silver, meaning that a variety of silver or silver-tipped projectiles could be used successfully against them. Silver daggers and the like could also theoretically be used, though the size and savagery of these creatures make close combat inadvisable. Hunters should ideally keep their distance and rely on ranged weapons.

In some accounts, wendigos are impervious to all forms of physical attack, including fire and silver. Should this prove accurate, and a hunter be completely unable to kill the monster before him, a hasty retreat would be required. There is no dishonor in this, and even the most ardent champion of traditional monster-hunting values would not expect one to face certain death against a beast that cannot be killed.

Summary

Dangers

- Teeth and claws
- Supernatural strength and speed
- Potential intangibility

Weaknesses

- Fire
- Silver

Selected Source

Colombo, John R., ed. *Windigo: An Anthology of Fact and Fantastic Fiction*. Saskatoon, Sask.: Western Producer Prairie Books, 1982. A collection of sources about the wendigo. (*Windigo* is a common alternate spelling.)

⋊ Werewolf ⋌

Description

A werewolf is a person who can (or is compelled to) transform into a large, lupine creature. Though some sources connect this metamorphosis with the appearance of the full moon, this is not included in the vast majority of folklore on the subject. Instead, the use of sorcery is a common cause of the transformation, and men turn into werewolves after dabbling with dark magic. These particular monsters can be found in the records of numerous cultures around the world, from ancient times to the present.

Werewolves, or lycanthropes, are fierce killers, swift and powerful. They are a suitable prey for skilled hunters, and often the cause of death for overly ambitious ones. As with vampires, they possess the fiendish ability to walk undetected among their potential victims, at least while in their human forms. Hence hunters might be able to find werewolves in almost any environment— from bustling cities to lonely forests. Whenever there is a spate of disappearances, or fatal animal attacks for which no culprit can be located, a hunter would be wise to investigate the area for werewolf activity.

Killing Methods

While conventional weapons of steel or wood are said to have no effect on werewolves, the werewolf's vulnerability to silver is well established and can be found in numerous historical cases from centuries ago. Silver-tipped arrows or crossbow bolts would hence be ideal weapons when hunting a werewolf, if they could be acquired.

A melee weapon such as a silver dagger could theoretically be used against a werewolf, though this is not recommended. The savage ferocity of a werewolf, its blend of brutal power and lupine agility, make it a considerable threat at close quarters. A hunter who casually engaged a werewolf with a bladed weapon might soon find his throat torn out by the beast's vicious teeth or claws.

Hunters who wish to avoid the expense of purchasing silver armaments, or who need to fight against a lycanthrope under emergency circumstances when no silver is at hand, can resort to fire. Flames are said to be able to wound and kill werewolves, meaning that flaming torches and the like could be employed to deal death to these creatures.

Pragmatic individuals wishing to eliminate a dangerous werewolf may consider the idea of tracking the monster down once it has reverted to its human form, and dispatching it then— when it may be vulnerable to all forms of harm, rather than merely fire and silver. Naturally, this would be rather unsportsmanlike, however, and earn one little respect among one's peers in the field of monster hunting.

Summary

Dangers

- Teeth
- Claws

Weaknesses

- Silver
- Fire

Selected Sources

Baring-Gould, Sabine. *The Book of Werewolves.* **Detroit: Omnigraphics, 1999.** A discussion of werewolf cases from ancient times onward.

Summers, Montague. *The Werewolf in Lore and Legend.* **New York: Dover, 2003.** A detailed examination of the werewolf.

Zombie

Description

A zombie is a reanimated corpse, the shell of a human being raised from the dead by dark rituals. Zombies are originally of Haitian origin, created through voodoo magic practiced there by a type of witch doctor known as a bokor. These sinister magicians often create zombies to carry out their bidding, which commonly involves attacking their enemies or thieving for them.

Killing Methods

A simple blade or arrow to a zombie's nonbeating heart is unlikely to stop the zombie. A more serious method, such as dismemberment or immolation, is probably called for. According to popular culture, zombies can also be dealt with via destruction of their brains, or severing of the brain stem. This seems plausible. Zombies demonstrate rudimentary intelligence, so their brains must be of some value to them. This is no doubt why older corpses, whose brains have experienced greater decay, cannot be reanimated. If one thus accepts that the brain is a viable target, then a wide variety of weapons could be taken on zombie hunts. Arrows or crossbow bolts could be used to pierce their brains. Greek fire or flaming torches could be used to burn them. Bladed weapons could be used to dismember or decapitate them.

Voodoo lore states that a zombie can be returned to its grave if it is made to taste salt, which is considered to be a symbol of white magic. Hence hurling salt at zombies may be a practical method of self-defense, albeit a far less satisfying one than hacking them apart.

Zombies can be among the most enjoyable creatures to hunt. While they are slow-witted, and their shambling forms lack the dexterity and quickness that might provide a challenge, they can often be found in packs. This means that a team of hunters can select their favorite weapons and spend all day massacring them in a variety of inventive ways.

There are some causes for caution on zombie hunts, however. Hunters should avoid being bitten by zombies. While there is nothing in the source material to support the idea that a person bitten by a zombie will become one himself, an undead creature is likely to have a rather unhygienic bite. Serious infections could result, which would clearly be undesirable. Hunters should also determine whether a bokor is nearby, issuing commands to the zombies. Their instructions may cause the zombies to fight more effectively, and hunters would hence be well advised to pick off the bokor first.

Summary

Dangers

- Possible infectious bite
- May be under the command of a bokor

Weakness

- Salt

Selected Source

Hurston, Zora Neale. *Tell My Horse: Voodoo and Life in Haiti and Jamaica.* **New York: Perennial, 1990, 179–98.** A discussion of various zombie cases, and the voodoo lore behind the phenomenon.

Part II
Enchanted Steel:
A Guide to Cryptohoplology

⊱ The Greatest of All ⊰ Treasures

Arma virumque cano . . . (I sing of arms and the man . . .)
—Virgil, *Aeneid* 1.1

It is impossible not to be fascinated by weapons and armor, mesmerized by the beautiful deadliness which gleams upon the blade of a sword or a spear, or entranced by the majestic strength of a well-crafted shield or cuirass. Yet while all weapons possess a certain magic, this work is concerned with those few pieces that rise above all others.

For millennia poets and bards have lovingly described the arms and armor with which the mightiest heroes carved out their place in legend—metal forged by supernatural forces, or otherwise imbued with abilities that mark them as superior to the weapons wielded by lesser men. Whether one is merely a collector of historical arms, or a monster hunter who desires to actually use these artifacts when hunting fearsome beasts, surely the thought of possessing such objects is tantalizing indeed.

This work will chronicle the most notable enchanted arms and armor that have emerged throughout the ages, providing a suitable introduction for those new to the field of cryptohoplology, and making readers aware of the descriptions and properties of these arcane artifacts. Such knowledge may assist treasure seekers in identifying their finds, and enable monster hunters to search for the items that best match their particular slaying needs. Wherever possible, information will be provided on the last known location of each item to provide a starting point for expeditions.

A Note on the Entries

The entries are arranged in alphabetical order. In the case of named weapons (e.g., Excalibur), the name is used as the entry title. For weapons or pieces of armor without names, the name of the object's owner (or the most notable owner for objects that have been through multiple hands) is used in the entry title (e.g., Heracles' Cloak). Where more than one relevant item is associated with a person, they are grouped together in a single entry (e.g., Aeneas's Arms and Armor).

Achilles' Armor
History and Description

When he went to war against the Trojans, Achilles was equipped with splendid armor. This was lost, however, after Hector stripped it from the corpse of Patroclus—to whom Achilles had lent it. Thus Achilles required a replacement before he could return to battle and avenge his friend. Knowing that her son was doomed to die, but determined that he should shine above all other men in his last days, the sea nymph Thetis brought Achilles armor forged on Olympus. Hephaestus himself, the god of blacksmiths, fashioned the armor in which Achilles would achieve his greatest victory and finally meet his death.

While Hephaestus made several other items to comprise the set—a corselet that is said to have shone brighter than a raging fire, an exquisite helmet topped with a ridge of pure gold, and a pair of greaves (leg armor)—the centerpiece was the shield. Huge and heavy, the fivefold shield (formed of two outer layers of bronze, two inner layers of tin, and a middle layer of gold) could absorb the mightiest blows. Even Aeneas, one of the greatest Trojan warriors, himself the son of a goddess, could pierce only the outer two layers. The blade of his spear could not penetrate the gold. Yet it was not merely the shield's defensive capabilities that filled men with awe; the engravings upon this glorious creation were breathtaking.

Since being aware of the exact nature of these distinctive engravings will allow one to correctly identify the genuine article if it is ever encountered, following is a comprehensive list of what it shows:

- The earth, sky, and sea
- The sun and waxing moon
- The constellations, including the Pleiades, the Hyades, Orion, and the Bear
- Two cities
  - In one there are weddings, feasts, and dancing. There is also a heated legal battle raging, with two men arguing over payment of blood money for a slaying.
  - The other city is under siege. The women, children, and old men are defending the walls, while the others are pouring forth to battle the besiegers. Their sortie is being led by Ares and Athena themselves, with the gods towering above the humans around them. The citizens are ambushing the enemy herdsmen, seizing their livestock. A bloody battle then ensues between the two armies.
- An agricultural scene, in which plowmen are working the land and taking a break to drink a cup of wine
- Laborers using sickles to reap a king's land, while others bind the fallen corn. The king watches, and his heralds prepare a feast.
- A vineyard, with young boys and girls carrying away the harvested grapes in baskets
- A herd of cattle being led by herdsmen. A pair of lions has killed one of the bulls at the back, and the beasts are busy feasting on it. The shepherds are trying to set the hounds on the lions, but the hounds will not comply.
- A pasture, with sheep pens and roofed huts
- A dance floor, on which numerous young men and women are reveling
- The ocean, around the edge of the shield

Clearly the shield is meant to depict the whole of Hellenic life. In some ways this is rather suitable, since Achilles is the greatest hero of the age, it is fitting that the whole world is carried on his shield. It is perhaps also poignant, since it depicts scenes of peace and tranquillity he will never see again—fated as he is to die in battle.

Following Achilles' death, the Achaean army debated whether his arms and armor should be awarded to Ajax or Odysseus—who were considered to be the greatest assets to the army after Achilles. Eventually it was decided that Odysseus would receive them. Considering this to be a great insult, and an immense show of disrespect from the Achaean kings, Ajax went insane and eventually killed himself. As with so many historical treasures, both glory and tragedy are present in the armor's tale. Odysseus did not keep this armor but presented it to Achilles' son Neoptolemus when he came to Troy to take his father's place. Neoptolemus survived the Trojan War and returned to Greece, so treasure hunters may wish to focus their attention there rather than upon the site of Troy (which is in modern-day Turkey).

Combative Applications

Achilles' divinely forged armor would provide excellent protection against the blades of men or centaurs. It would adequately defend the wearer's flesh from the fangs or claws of beasts. In addition, the intense brightness exuded by the corselet might serve to blind attackers and perhaps frighten away less intelligent monsters. When trespassing in a dragon's cave or a vampire's crypt, it also could make a useful substitute for a torch, enabling the wearer to see clearly without the added encumbrance of carrying a source of light in his hand. However, this corselet would obviously not be suitable for any stealthy endeavor. A person wearing it would be far too visible, and could not hope to surreptitiously track a creature through dark woods, for example. Furthermore, if it truly is as bright as legend recounts, it would be advisable for the wearer to avoid walking near mirrors, lest the reflected light blind him.

The shield would likewise be a protective device, though of course the natural drawback of shields is the fact that carrying one encumbers the user's arm, limiting what can be done with that limb. In addition, one might be reluctant to have its wonderfully artistic surface marred by use in battle. As Aeneas's piercing of the top two layers demonstrates, the shield—or at least its outer layers—are not impenetrable. An extremely powerful thrust will pierce the metal.

Selected Sources

Homer. *Iliad* 18.478–618. A description of the armor being crafted by Hephaestus, including the details of the engravings on the shield; **20.258–72.** Aeneas thrusts his spear at Achilles' shield, but it will not penetrate beyond the second layer of bronze.

Quintus of Smyrna. *Fall of Troy* 5.121–332. The quarrel over the fate of Achilles' arms, which are awarded to Odysseus; **6.193–212.** Odysseus tells Neoptolemus that he will give him Achilles' equipment if he comes to Troy.

⇢⊸ Aegis ⊷⇠

History and Description

The aegis, a tasseled cloak, was frequently worn or carried by Zeus or Athena. Different sources attribute different origins to this artifact. Some say that Athena skinned a Titan named Pallas during one of the great celestial wars, and crafted armor from his skin. Others claim that the aegis was created when Zeus skinned the supernatural goat that had suckled him. While these multiple versions may indicate confusion among ancient writers as to the true story, it is also possible that there was more than one aegis— and that more than one origin is therefore correct.

The two gods used the aegis as both a weapon and a means of protection. When they shook it, men would flee in uncontrollable fear. When they wore it as armor, it offered superb protection. During the Trojan War, Ares, bloodthirsty god of war, attacked Athena on the plains of Troy as the gods took sides and battled with one another. His spear, despite all the berserk force behind it, was not able to pierce her aegis. It is said that not even Zeus's divine thunderbolts could penetrate it.

Athena draped the aegis around Achilles' shoulders after he had lost his armor and hence was unable to immediately charge into battle, avenge his friend Patroclus, and turn back the Trojan tide. Wearing the aegis enabled him to cause mass confusion among the Trojans simply by screaming his war cry. This is significant, since it demonstrates that the powers of the aegis can be used by men as well as by gods.

While the aegis may be on Olympus, and therefore beyond the reach of treasure hunters, one may wish to scour the major temples of Athena and Zeus, or the museums and private collections that have appropriated artifacts from these locations. Sacred items were often left in temples, from which an industrious seeker of enchanted arms could liberate them.

Combative Applications

The impressive resilience of the aegis would make it perhaps the greatest piece of armor one could possess. If it can withstand a thunderbolt or the war god's spear, then it would surely stand up to anything a human or even a monster could throw at it. In addition, since it is a cloak, it would weigh less than a metal cuirass, and could be used in a greater variety of ways. One might wish to wear it on the torso, or perhaps wrap it around one's arm as a shield. However, while the aegis will likely defend against all forms of piercing damage, blunt trauma may still harm the wearer. The material itself may be impervious to harm, but some of the force of a powerful clubbing blow may still be passed on to the flesh and bone beneath it.

The ability to strike fear into enemies by shaking the aegis would, of course, also be extremely valuable. If suddenly attacked by a dangerous monster, for example, at a time when one is unprepared to fight it, the aegis could be used to repel the creature.

Selected Sources

Apollodorus. *Library* **1.6.2.**
Athena flays Pallas and uses his skin as armor.

Homer. *Iliad* **15.306–27.** Zeus lends his aegis to Apollo, who uses it to strike fear into the Achaean army; **18.202–18**. Athena drapes the aegis around Achilles' shoulders, and his war cry causes chaos among the Trojans; **21.400–8**. Ares strikes Athena with his spear, but her aegis stops the blow, allowing her to casually pick up a boulder and knock him to the ground with it.

Hyginus. *Astronomica* **2.13.** Two versions of a myth—one in which Zeus skins the goat that suckled him to create the aegis, and one in which he skins the goat belonging to the nymph who suckled him.

❧ Aeneas's Arms ❧
and Armor
History and Description

Following the destruction of Troy, the Trojan prince Aeneas sailed to Italy, where he was fated to found the Roman race. However, he found himself once again in the midst of a brutal conflict, as the indigenous Latin people became his enemies and waged war against him. To aid her son in these battles, the goddess Venus had Vulcan— her husband, and the god of blacksmithing—forge arms for him.

The set Vulcan created included a helmet that belched forth flames. There was a blood-red bronze corselet upon which regular weapons would break or be turned aside. Even Turnus, the mightiest of all Aeneas's foes, could not pierce it. There was a death-dealing sword and a spear, which Aeneas would use to slay many Latins before the hostilities ended, and greaves made of valuable gold and electrum to protect his legs. As with Achilles' arms, however, the centerpiece was an exquisitely engraved shield.

The shield, crafted by a deity who could see events in the distant future, depicted the entire sweep of Roman history. To aid in the correct identification of this object, here is a full list of specific events that are recorded as appearing on the shield:

- The she-wolf suckling Romulus and Remus, the legendary twin sons of Mars who would found Rome in 753 B.C.
- The rape of the Sabine women that Romulus instigated, the subsequent war, and the eventual reconciliation between the two sides.

- The execution of Mettus Fufetius, dictator of Alba Longa. He was tied to chariots that were then sent in opposite directions, tearing his body in half. His bloody corpse is shown being dragged through brambles. He had made a treaty with Tullus Hostilius, the third king of Rome, then deserted him in battle.
- Scenes of battle from the Etruscan attack on Rome in 508 B.C.
- The attack of the Gauls in 390 B.C., the attempt made by the Gauls to seize the Capitol under the cover of night, and its thwarting when the sacred geese of Juno honked and alerted the Romans.
- A scene showing the good being rewarded and the bad being punished in the underworld.
- The center, surrounded by a ring of dolphins, shows Augustus's victory over Antony and Cleopatra at Actium in 31 B.C. The mortal navies clash while the gods of each nation (Rome and Egypt) fight above them. With this is shown Augustus's triple triumph of 29 B.C. His procession marches through the streets of Rome, to much celebration and fanfare.

It is unknown what became of Aeneas's arms following the founding of his city. Italy would obviously be the logical place to begin searching for them, though it is possible they were looted and taken elsewhere. Aeneas was deified following the events chronicled in the *Aeneid*, so he might have taken the arms to Olympus with him.

Combative Applications

Aeneas's armor can resist the most powerful blows from conventional weapons. When Turnus attacked him with a regular sword, it broke against Aeneas's corselet. The outer layers of the shield, on the other hand, can be penetrated by powerful attacks. When Mezentius hurled javelins at Aeneas, they became embedded there. The fact that the spears did not pierce all the way through testifies to the shield's protective power. Hence the shield and armor would be priceless assets to any warrior or monster hunter. In addition, the shield is described at one point as emitting flame, though this does not appear to be part of its usual properties. It merely happened once, as Aeneas's ship approached the shore where his people were under siege, and his enemies and allies caught sight of him—filling the former with fear and the latter with hope. It is possible that this ability is mentally activated, and occurs only when one subconsciously feels that it would enhance the drama of the situation at hand.

The flame-spurting helmet, on the other hand, probably displays this power on a regular basis—since it is described as possessing the property when it is first spoken of in the epic accounts, as well as in the aforementioned incident on the ship. This flame could perhaps be used to burn one's foes, though there is no indication that this fire can be directed. It would serve as a useful source of light when investigating darkened caves, for example, though it might prove to be a liability if worn in a wooded area or indoors. Should the flame set things alight, the area around the wearer could quickly become a raging inferno. Also, the presence of a heat source atop one's head could make one uncomfortably hot.

The sword and the spear are not recorded as possessing any specific powers, though they appear able to cut through flesh and armor rather easily. They would perhaps be effective against enchanted armor as well, though this cannot be confirmed.

Selected Source

Virgil. *Aeneid.* **8.617–731.** A description of the arms, including a detailed account of the images on the shield; **10.270–75.** Aeneas's helmet and shield pour forth fire; **10.328–32, 882–87.** Spears tend to bounce off the shield, and even when thrown by a powerful warrior such as Mezentius, they will merely stick in the shield rather than penetrate all the way through; **12.728–41.** Turnus strikes at Aeneas, and Turnus's sword breaks. He realizes that he has picked up his charioteer's sword rather than his own, and that a normal weapon is unable to penetrate the divine armor.

✎✦ Blue Blade ✦✎

History and Description

During the period of the Three Kingdoms in ancient Chinese history, the country was split into three major dominions, each ruled by a powerful dynasty—Wu, Shu, and Wei. The king of Wei, who held the northern regions, was named Cao Cao. This cunning and often treacherous general possessed two magic swords—Blue Blade and Trust of God. Though the latter was the one he personally wore, and was therefore perhaps the more powerful of the two, little is known about what magical properties it may have been endowed with. Writings concerning Blue Blade, however, reveal what that weapon was capable of. It is said that the azure-bladed sword bore the sharpest edge of any weapon, and was able to cut through iron as if it were mud. Nothing could stand up to its edge.

Blue Blade was customarily carried in battle by Xiahou En, Cao Cao's sword-bearer. He wore it slung across his back as a symbol of his office and authority. He likely did not wield it himself, but rather kept it ready to hand to his lord when Cao Cao required its unstoppable edge. However, Xiahou En ultimately failed in his duty, and lost the sword he had been entrusted with—along with his life. The great Shu warrior Zhao Yun (also known as Zhao Zilong) encountered Xiahou En while the sword-bearer and ten of his cavalrymen were riding around and plundering in Wei's name. Zhao Yun rode straight toward Xiahou En, disarmed him, and knocked him from his horse. The other cavalrymen promptly fled, fearful of this powerful warrior. Zhao Yun slew the sword-bearer, and examined the weapon he carried on his back. Gold letters were written across it,

proclaiming the name Blue Blade. Realizing that this was Cao Cao's legendary sword, Zhao Yun took it.

The Shu warrior would soon be provided with the opportunity to test out Blue Blade's magical edge. Shortly after killing Xiahou En, he came across his lord Liu Bei's infant son, whom he was determined to reunite with his father—despite the countless Wei warriors who stood between him and Shu territory. Zhao Yun loosened the armor on his torso and put the baby inside it, held in place against his chest. Then he rode toward Liu Bei as dozens of Wei soldiers were sent against him. On that day Zhao Yun demonstrated why many consider him to have been the greatest warrior of the age. He slaughtered waves of Wei troops, all the while protecting the child from their blows. During the carnage, he came up against Zhong Shen, one of Cao Cao's generals. Zhao Yun lashed out at him with Blue Blade, and the enchanted sword cleaved through both helmet and skull— completely shearing off the top of his head, and sending it tumbling to the ground. With the unstoppable weapon in his hand, Zhao Yun succeeded against seemingly impossible odds and managed to bring the child to Liu Bei.

Zhao Yun was the longest-lived of Liu Bei's Tiger Generals. Unequaled in battle, he died of old age rather than to the weapons of his enemies. It is unknown what became of Blue Blade, though those searching for it would be well advised to start in China—perhaps focusing on the most ancient shrines, where such a weapon may have been placed.

Combative Applications

Being able to cut through iron as if it were mud would naturally be useful, and this piercing power would presumably translate to most forms of armor—whether man-made metal or the scaled hides of monsters. Blue Blade would enable a warrior to bring down almost any foe, no matter how well protected.

The weapon was sometimes known as the Sword of Light or Luminous Sword. This perhaps indicates that the blade is not merely tinted blue, but actually emits a vibrant azure glow. Such an effect would no doubt be attractive, and could perhaps be used to frighten away less intelligent beasts.

Selected Source

Luo Guanzhong. *Romance of the Three Kingdoms,* Vol. 2. Trans. Robert Moss. Beijing: Foreign Language Press, 1991, 735–42.
Zhao Yun acquires Blue Blade and rescues Liu Bei's son.

⤞⤙ Durendal ⤚⤝

History and Description

The legendary knight Roland wielded the sword Durendal during his many battles against the Saracens in the latter half of the eighth century and used it to slay countless enemies. Though the sword bore a golden hilt, its greatest treasures lay underneath this layer of finery, for inside were holy relics—a thread from the Virgin Mary's dress, one of St. Peter's teeth, some of St. Basil's blood, and strands of St. Denis's hair.

When he lay dying after his last heroic fight. Roland attempted to break Durendal's blade with a rock, lest the sword be taken and wielded by the Saracens. However, he found that the blade was indestructible, and would not yield no matter how hard he struck it.

It is uncertain what became of Durendal following Roland's death. France and Spain would be the logical starting points for a treasure seeker attempting to locate and recover this weapon.

Combative Applications

Having an indestructible sword could be a tremendous asset, since an unbreakable blade may be able to penetrate the hides of heavily armored monsters—against which regular swords would likely shatter. In addition, the relics contained in the hilt may give the weapon the status of a holy object, allowing it to cause increased damage against undead creatures such as vampires or mummies.

Selected Source

Song of Roland **verse 83.** Roland promises to bloody his sword up to the gold, indicating that the hilt is golden; **Verse 171–3**. Roland tries to break Durendal but fails. He then recounts what he has achieved with the sword, and speaks of the relics contained in it.

✺ Excalibur ✺
History and Description

When a sword embedded in a rock appeared in London, with writing on it promising that only the rightful king of England could remove the weapon, it understandably attracted a great deal of attention. Knights came from across the land to attempt this feat and gain the throne. All failed until Arthur yanked it free—hoping to provide his brother with the weapon, in place of his own, which he had neglected to bring with him. Thus Arthur began one of the most famous monarchical reigns in history or legend.

However, the sword from the stone was far from being a perfect weapon. In fact, it broke in combat when the blade was struck a heavy blow by another sword. To replace this now useless weapon, the wizard Merlin took Arthur to a lake. Protruding from this expanse of water was a sword being held by a woman—the Lady of the Lake (though it would later emerge that she was but one of many ladies of the lake). The king rowed out to the weapon and asked her to furnish him with it. She agreed, on condition that he grant her a favor in return at some point in the future. Arthur gave his word that he would do so, and accepted the weapon.

The sword was housed in a scabbard covered with gold and encrusted with jewels—surely a most valuable treasure. The sword itself was also finely adorned, with numerous precious stones set in the pommel and hilt. Hence it must not have seemed strange when Merlin asked Arthur which he valued more—the sword or the scabbard. Arthur, a pragmatic and martial ruler, replied that he preferred the sword. Merlin chided him for his foolishness and informed him that the scabbard was magical. While Arthur carried it, his wounds—no matter how grievous—would never bleed.

Later the Lady of the Lake came to Arthur's court. She told him the name of the weapon she had given him—Excalibur—and demanded that he grant her a favor, as he had promised to do. He agreed to honor his promise, and asked her what she desired. She responded by demanding the life of Balin, a knight who had recently arrived at court. Arthur refused, and offered to do something else for her instead. Yet she remained firm, placing the king in a difficult position. He had to choose between committing an unjust killing or breaking his oath. Fortunately, the matter was taken out of his hands when Balin appeared and decapitated the lady. While Arthur was horrified by this, and banished Balin, it certainly solved Arthur's problem. He bestowed a lavish funeral on her by way of a settling of his debt.

Though he would wield the sword until his life drew near its end, Arthur lost the scabbard. The evil sorceress Morgan Le Fey stole it from his bedchamber and hurled it into a lake—where it promptly sank beneath the weight of the gold and gemstones. Thus its magic was not present to save his life in his final battle, against the forces of his illegitimate son Mordred, after which Arthur lay mortally wounded. As his final request, he asked one of his knights—Sir Bedivere—to hurl Excalibur into a nearby lake. Bedivere agreed, though had second thoughts after he left the dying king's sight. Thinking it a shame to cast away such a fine weapon, he hid the sword and told Arthur that he had done as commanded. However, when Arthur asked what had happened after he threw the sword into the lake, Bedivere's answer did not satisfy him. He knew that the knight was trying to deceive him. After one final attempt at deception, Bedivere finally obeyed his king's order and hurled the sword out onto the water—where it was caught by the hand of another Lady of the Lake.

According to the source material, it therefore seems likely that Excalibur and the scabbard can be found in two different lakes somewhere in England, unless one of the eldritch women who dwell in the lakes recovered the scabbard, in which case both would likely be found in the same body of water. While a treasure seeker with diving experience may be able to acquire the scabbard fairly easily once the correct lake has been found, assuming that it has not been recovered and reunited with the sword, obtaining Excalibur could prove more difficult. The Lady of the Lake who gave it to Arthur only did so in return for a favor—one which proved to be rather terrible and malign. Hence someone who desired to possess the weapon, even if the Lady of the Lake was willing to hand it over to him, may later be faced with a moral dilemma. To acquire Excalibur, a dark favor may be a necessary price.

Combative Applications

Though apparently a fine sword that could cut well and remain sturdy and strong through countless battles, there does not seem to be anything particularly exceptional about Excalibur itself. The scabbard, on the other hand, would be a great aid to any warrior or monster hunter. While it is, of course, possible to die without losing blood (e.g., if one is incinerated by a monster's flaming breath, or if one's neck is broken by a powerful blow), possessing the scabbard would at least remove the danger of bleeding to death after a brutal fight and reduce the severity of any wounds sustained.

Selected Source

Malory, Sir Thomas. *Le Morte D'Arthur* **1.5.** Arthur pulls the sword from the stone; **1.23.** The sword from the stone breaks in combat; **1.25.** Arthur obtains a new sword in return for promising to perform a favor for the Lady of the Lake. Merlin informs him of the scabbard's power; **2.3.** The Lady of the Lake's arrives at Arthur's court, names the sword, and asks Arthur to kill Balin to fulfill his promise to her. She is subsequently killed by Balin; **4.14.** Morgan Le Fey steals Excalibur's scabbard and hurls it into a lake. The scabbard is described as being covered with gold and encrusted with jewels; **21.5.** Arthur asks Bedivere to cast Excalibur into a lake. After trying and failing to deceive him, Bedivere complies. A hand reaches up to catch it, and drags it under. The pommel and the hilt of the sword are described as being covered with precious stones.

⚜ Fragarach ⚜

History and Description

The Celtic hero Lugh possessed the sword Fragarach (the Answerer), one of the treasures of the Tuatha Dé Danaan people. Its blade could pierce any armor, and it is said that whoever was wounded by it would die—though whether this inevitable death was the result of poison or a magical curse associated with this weapon is not specified. In addition, when Fragarach was drawn, it would bewitch those it was turned against, draining their strength and leaving them as weak and vulnerable as women in childbirth (though one wonders at this curious analogy made in the sources, since childbirth could logically be seen as the moment at which a woman's strength is greatest).

It is unknown where this sword currently resides, though Ireland would be a logical starting point for treasure seekers hunting for this legendary Celtic artifact.

Combative Applications

Given its ability to penetrate through armor (though this may not apply to enchanted armor) and bring death with a single cut, Fragarach would be an exceptional weapon against monsters. It could get through the tough hides of the more heavily protected creatures one might face, and dispatch them even if it did not strike a critical location. The fact that the mere presence of the sword drains the strength of one's enemies makes the weapon even more impressive. Powerful adversaries would have their might negated, making it easier for Fragarach's wielder to strike the single blow necessary to slaughter them.

Selected Sources

Gregory, Lady Augusta. *Gods and Fighting Men: The Story of the Tuatha Dé Danaan and of the Fianna of Ireland.* London: John Murray, 1913, 22. The properties of Fragarach—how it drains the strength of those it is raised against, and will always kill whomever it wounds.

Rolleston, Thomas. *Myths and Legends of the Celtic Race.* London: Harrap, 1911, 112. Fragarach is said to be able to cut through any armor.

⛧ Gáe Bulga ⛧
History and Description

The Gáe Bulga was a spear used by the Celtic hero Cúchulainn.
When thrown into an enemy's body, the formerly smooth spear shaft
would suddenly be covered in long barbs, which would tear apart the
victim's insides. Due to the number of barbs, and the extent of their
penetration, the Gáe Bulga would become firmly embedded in the
victim's body. It could not be pulled free, but instead had to be cut
loose from the surrounding flesh. Once the spear was cut from a
corpse, the barbs could presumably be retracted for later use.

Curiously, the sources say that Cúchulainn threw the Gáe
Bulga from "the fork of his foot" rather than his hand. This
presumably means that he held it between his big toe and second
toe, and somehow managed to launch it from such a position.

Combative Applications

The Gáe Bulga could be used to cause grievous wounds to a
target. Once it penetrated, the expanding barbs would brutally tear
through the surrounding area, so that even a minor wound would
soon become a mortal one, or at least cause severe maiming. This
would be useful against large monsters, which would normally be
able to survive several spears being hurled into them. The barbs
would lacerate their vulnerable organs, and even the hardiest
creature could be eviscerated by a single weapon.

While the Gáe Bulga was apparently thrown from the foot
rather than the hand, the development of such a skill sounds to be
more trouble than it would be worth. Logically it should also be
possible to hurl the weapon from one's hand.

Selected Source

Dunn, Joseph. *The Ancient Irish Epic Tale Táin Bó Cúalnge.*
London: David Nutt, 1914, chapter 15. Cúchulainn battles Ferdiad, and eventually kills him with the Gáe Bulga.

❧ Gram ❧

History and Description

During a great wedding feast at the house of the Norse king Volsung, a mysterious one-eyed stranger entered the hall. He drew a sword and plunged it into the tree trunk around which the hall was built. The stranger, in truth the god Odin in disguise, declared that whoever pulled it free could keep it, and that they would find it to be a most excellent blade. Then he left, and disappeared into the night.

There were many mighty warriors at the feast, and each of them hurried forth to pull the weapon free. But it remained firm, no matter how hard they yanked at it. Then Sigmund, son of King Volsung, stepped to the tree trunk. He set his hand on the sword's hilt and drew it out. All those present marveled at the weapon, which was the finest they had ever seen. King Siggeir of Gothland offered three times the sword's weight in gold if Sigmund would sell it to him, though Sigmund refused—leading to a great feud between their families that would result in much bloodshed.

In his old age, King Sigmund decided to ask for the hand of Hjördis, daughter of King Eylimi; Hjördis was said to be the wisest woman in all the lands. However, another king, Lyngi, had the same idea. Faced with two suitors for his daughter, Eylimi asked Hjördis to choose between them. She chose Sigmund to be her husband. Furious at this slight, Lyngi assembled an army and made ready to attack Sigmund. The ensuing battle was to be Sigmund's last. He fought valiantly, and slaughtered many enemies on the field. None of them could stand before the sword he had drawn from the tree trunk, Gram, which would

slice through shields and armor, flesh and bone. But then he encountered a one-eyed stranger on the field. For his own inscrutable purposes, Odin had decided that Sigmund's tenure as wielder of the sword should end. Sigmund struck at Odin, but the god parried, and the sword broke in two. At that moment the tide of battle turned. Sigmund's forces were defeated, and he was mortally wounded.

On his deathbed, Sigmund entrusted the pieces of the sword to Hjördis, and told her that the blade was destined to be reforged, and wielded by the child who grew in her womb. Thus she kept them safe until the day when Sigurd—their son, born after his father's death—was ready to receive them.

Years later, when he had come of age, Sigurd wished to kill the dragon Fafnir, who guarded a horde of treasure. Regin, a skilled blacksmith, offered to make him a sword capable of piercing the dragon's hide. He forged a sword, and Sigurd tested it by striking an anvil. The sword broke, and Sigurd asked him to make a better one. Regin did so, though once again the sword broke when Sigurd struck it against an anvil. Thus it was that Sigurd went to his mother and asked for the pieces of Gram. Hjördis gave them to him, and Regin reforged the weapon. Once it was finished, Sigurd took the sword and again struck an anvil with it. This time the blade cleaved through the metal and remained undamaged. Finally Sigurd had his blade, which he would carry until the day of his death. With it he slaughtered many enemies and slew the dragon.

Combative Applications

A sword that can cut through an anvil can surely cleave through even the toughest scales. It could be used to slay any monster vulnerable to conventional weapons, regardless of how thick or how hard its hide was. Given the sword's exceptional toughness, and the fact that it was not even chipped when struck against an anvil, it could perhaps also be used to chop through barricades such as steel doors or brick walls.

One note of caution: Gram broke when Sigmund used it to attack Odin. While this may be because Odin had a special power over the weapon, since it was originally in his possession, it also may indicate that the weapon is unsuitable for battling gods in general. Hence monster hunters wishing to commit deicide would perhaps be better served by one of the other weapons described in this work.

Selected Source

The Volsung Saga **3.** Sigmund pulls Gram from the tree trunk; **11–12.** The sword is broken in battle, and Hjördis is instructed to keep the pieces for their son; **15.** Gram is reforged and cleaves through an anvil; **18.** Sigurd uses Gram to slay the dragon Fafnir.

⚓ Hades' Helmet ⚓
History and Description

Hades, god of the underworld, possessed a helmet that would turn the wearer invisible. When wearing it, the dread god of death could walk among men or gods as though shrouded in complete darkness. He could go where he pleased, with those around him little suspecting the powerful presence that passed among them.

Hades often lent this helm to his fellow gods. Hermes wore it during the celestial war between the gods and giants, and Athena used it at Troy, when she wished to surreptitiously arrange for Ares to be wounded by the hero Diomedes. On occasion Hades even allowed mortals to wear his helmet on their adventures. In some ancient sources Perseus is said to have worn it when he killed Medusa.

Unlike certain other Hellenic deities, Hades did not possess numerous temples in which to store his treasures. Hence the helmet is most likely in the underworld. This does not make it completely unobtainable, as attested to by the stories of heroes such as Heracles and Odysseus journeying into that foreboding realm and managing to return to the surface, though it means that only the most courageous and daring treasure seekers would be able to retrieve it.

Combative Applications

Being invisible, able to deal death in broad daylight while staying completely anonymous, is surely a feature that would appeal to any assassin. While monster hunters may find such tactics unsuitable for their own trade, since it seems rather unsporting,

the helmet would nevertheless provide a useful emergency device for escaping after a failed attempt to slay a powerful beast.

Of course, one would have to be cautious when using this device, and not become overly complacent. The sweeping flame of a dragon's breath would be quite capable of eliminating an invisible enemy, even if the dragon was not precisely sure where that enemy was. Certain environmental factors—for example, rain—also would reveal the location of a person wearing the helmet.

Selected Sources

Apollodorus. *Library* **1.6.2.** Hermes wears the helmet while killing a giant; **2.4.2.** Perseus uses it while killing Medusa.

Homer. *Iliad* **5.844–63.** Athena dons the helmet so she can subtly help Diomedes wound Ares.

✵ Heracles' Cloak ✵

History and Description

As the first of the hero's fabled twelve labors, Heracles was commanded to slay the fearsome Nemean lion. Thus he tracked the beast, and upon locating it he attempted to bring it down with his arrows. Yet though his arrows would slaughter many a foe during his illustrious career, they merely bounced off the lion's tough hide. Fearless even in the face of this setback, Heracles charged the lion, and smashed his club against the creature's skull. The club broke against the monster's impervious skin, though the force of the blow stunned the lion. Quickly seizing the advantage, Heracles grabbed the groggy beast and strangled it to death with a wrestling hold.

Impressed with the resilience of the beast's hide, Heracles decided to skin the creature. Naturally, the concept of skinning a creature with a seemingly impenetrable hide raised an obvious difficulty. However, the lion's own claws could pierce its skin. Hence Heracles was able to fashion a cloak, with the monster's head forming the hood. He wore this armor throughout his remaining adventures.

Following the end of his earthly life, Heracles was deified and taken up to Olympus to dwell among the gods. If he took the lion's pelt with him, then acquiring it would be impossible. If he left it behind, it may still be somewhere in Greece.

Combative Applications

Completely impenetrable to conventional weapons, and a light garment rather than a weighty construction of metal, the skin of the Nemean lion has tremendous value as a piece of armor. It would offer superb protection and be versatile. It could be wrapped around one's arm in lieu of a shield, for example, in addition to being worn in the usual fashion.

However, Heracles could stun the lion with his club—albeit at the cost of the weapon. While the cloak will protect the wearer from piercing attacks, it will not completely protect against the impact caused by blunt trauma.

Selected Source

Theocritus. *Idyll* **25.153–281.** Heracles' battle with the Nemean lion, and his subsequent skinning of the creature.

⊱ Kusanagi ⊰
History and Description

When the Japanese god Sosa no wo no Mikoto was visiting the Ye River in the province of Aki, he came upon a divine couple who were locked in sorrow. Sosa no wo learned that the goddess was pregnant and would soon give birth to a child. This caused them much grief, since each of their many previous offspring had been devoured by an eight-headed serpent, despite their best efforts at fending off this beast. Eager to rectify this long-standing injustice, Sosa no wo told the deities that if they obeyed his instructions he would deal with the great serpent. He commanded them to gather a variety of fruits, as many as they could find, and make eight jars of wine from them. The two gods did so, though they must have found his orders strange indeed.

When it was time for the goddess to give birth, the eight-headed serpent arrived to devour her child. However, Sosa no wo intercepted the monster and made it an offering of wine. He set each of the eight jars before one of its heads, and the serpent eagerly drained them all. Full of the potent wine, the creature fell asleep. Sosa no wo drew his sword and dispatched the creature while it slept. He hacked at the beast's heads and its long necks. Yet when he tried to sever its tail, his sword met something unyielding, which left a slight notch on the blade. Curious, the god split open the serpent's tail to see what was inside. He found a sword hidden within the reptilian flesh, which became known as Murakumo. Sensing that the sword before him was divine and carried great power, he decided that it would be unseemly for him to bear it. Instead he offered it to the heavenly gods. The gods did not keep Murakumo, however. They sent it back to the

mortals to become part of the Japanese regalia. Thus Murakumo became a symbol of imperial power.

When Prince Yamato-Dake set out to quash a great rebellion, the emperor of Japan gave him the divine blade to wield, for it was the finest weapon in all the land. This proved to be a fortuitous decision, for the sword saved the prince's life when the rebels set fire to the foliage around him, threatening to burn him to death in a raging inferno. Murakumo leaped into the air of its own accord, and slashed away the nearby bushes. The prince was able to escape, and from that day forth the sword took on the name Kusanagi (Grass-cutter). Yamato-Dake went on to slaughter the rebels with Kusanagi at his side.

While the modern Japanese regalia still contains a sword, this is a mere replica. The original Kusanagi was lost in 1185 at the Battle of Dan-no-ura, a major naval battle of the Genpei War. The child-emperor Antoku was drowned, and Kusanagi was lost in the bloody waters. Treasure hunters searching for the sword would be advised to begin their search for the weapon at the site of this famous battle.

Combative Applications

Kusanagi was a fine blade, capable of notching the sword of a god. However, its true power surely is that it could wield itself to save Yamato-Dake's life. If the sword can fight and kill without needing to be held, it would provide an additional means of attacking one's enemies, in conjunction with whichever other weapon or weapons are held in one's hands. It also could act as a means of defense, floating around and intercepting attacks. When facing a supremely dangerous monster, one that could not be safely fought at close quarters, Kusanagi could be sent in to slay the beast. The sword's herbicidal tendencies may also make it an asset in the garden.

Selected Sources

Shoi Nihon. *Nihongi: Chronicles of Japan from the Earliest Times to A.D. 697.* **Trans. W. G. Aston. Tokyo: Tuttle, 1972, 52–58.** Different accounts of how Sosa no wo no Mikoto killed a great serpent and discovered Kusanagi in its tail; **76.** Kusanagi becomes part of the Japanese regalia; **205.** The tale of how Kusanagi acquired its name.

Turnball, Stephen. *Samurai: The Warrior Tradition.* **London: Arms & Armour Press, 1996, 26.** Kusanagi is lost following the Battle of Dan-no-ura.

⚜ Mjolnir ⚜
History and Description

Loki, the roguish trickster of the Norse pantheon, cut off Sif's golden hair for his own personal amusement. However, this was a poorly conceived jape, since Sif happened to be married to Thor, the mighty god of thunder. Thor promptly seized Loki and prepared to break every bone in his body. Loki hastily told Thor that he could have the dwarfs make new hair for Sif—out of enchanted gold that would be just like her former hair, and grow as normal. Thor agreed to this, and Loki visited the dwarfs.

The dwarf smiths Sindri and Brokkr created the hair, as well as other fine items for the gods—including Gungnir, the spear that would be wielded by Odin, head of the Norse pantheon. Impressed with the quality of these items and seeing a chance to create more mischief, Loki made a bet with the smiths. He claimed that they would not be able to create three other enchanted items of equal value to those they had already made. The dwarfs accepted the challenge and set to work.

Sindri prepared the first item, and laid it in the hearth. He instructed Brokkr to work the bellows and blow on it until he returned, and then left the room. Anxious to win the bet (since he had wagered his own head for some bizarre reason), Loki transformed himself into a fly and began to bite Brokkr's hand— hoping to disrupt his working of the bellows and ruin the object. However, Brokkr worked through the discomfort, and when Sindri returned, he removed a living boar with golden bristles from the hearth. Sindri then prepared the second item, and again left after instructing Brokkr to blow on it until he returned. This time

Loki began to bite Brokkr's neck, in the hope of sabotaging the work. Once again, however, the dwarf persevered. When Sindri returned, he took a golden ring named Draupnir from the hearth. Pleased with his work thus far, Sindri laid the third and final item down, and as before, instructed Brokkr to keep blowing on it until he returned. Having been thwarted in his attempts to ruin the previous two items, Loki was desperate. This time he bit Brokkr above the eye, and the blood from the wound trickled down and obscured the dwarf's vision. Brokkr instinctively raised his hand to his eye to wipe away the blood, and the bellows fell flat. Sindri returned to see that his work had been damaged. The great war hammer Mjolnir, destined to be the weapon of Thor, had ended up with an overly short handle.

Despite this setback, Sindri told Brokkr to take their creations to the rest of the Aesir pantheon. Upon seeing the amazing artifacts laid before them, the gods agreed that the dwarfs had won the bet. Even with the shortness of the hammer's handle, they declared that it was the greatest of all the treasures, and awarded it to Thor, that he might use it to battle against the giants. Loki was told that he would have to surrender his head, in accordance with the terms of his wager. Loki promptly ran away, only to be caught and dragged back by Thor. However, in his desperate cunning Loki came up with a solution to his predicament. He informed his audience that he had only wagered his head, not his neck—and that any attempt to remove the former would count as illegitimate if it harmed the latter. The gods agreed that this was so. Hence instead of decapitating Loki, Brokkr sewed his mouth shut.

The war hammer Mjolnir was a powerful weapon indeed. It would never break, no matter how hard it was smashed against objects or victims. If Thor threw it, the hammer would never miss, and would always return to his grasp. With this potent tool in his hand, the god of thunder slaughtered countless giants.

Since Thor is supposedly destined to battle the Midgard Serpent during the Norse apocalypse, it stands to reason that he keeps the hammer with him at all times in preparation for that day. Hence the only way it might be acquired is if a bold and determined treasure seeker lurked around Scandinavia or Iceland during thunderstorms, located Thor, and surreptitiously stole it. In addition to the great risk involved in such an endeavor, however, without Mjolnir Thor would most likely not be able to slay the Midgard Serpent. This could have a catastrophic effect on the balance of power in those most dangerous times.

Combative Applications

Mjolnir is surely powerful enough to smash the bones of even the hardiest monsters, and can be used at close quarters or hurled at a distant foe. Thus it would provide an all-purpose weapon, allowing the wielder to fight in a melee or from range. The fact that the hammer will always return to the user means that it could be greatly relied upon. Even if he found himself disarmed, or stumbled and dropped the weapon, the wielder could rest assured that the hammer would come back to his hand.

The one problem is that Mjolnir is most likely an extremely heavy weapon—designed to break the bones and crush the skulls of giants. This, combined with the limited leverage provided by the short handle, would perhaps make it unusable for most people.

Selected Sources

Sturlson, Snorri. *The Prose Edda: Gylfaginning* **51.** In end-times Thor will slay the Midgard Serpent, then walk a mere nine paces before succumbing to the great snake's venom.

———.*The Prose Edda: Skaldskaparmal* **35.** Loki's wager and the making of Mjolnir.

⚜ Paracelsus's Sword ⚜
History and Description

While one might not be naturally inclined to associate swords with a famous alchemist such as Paracelsus, he allegedly kept his weapon by his side at all times—even when he slept. A possible explanation for this strange behavior may be revealed by sixteenth-century portraits of Paracelsus. He was depicted holding his sword, and the word *azoth* was shown inscribed on its pommel.

Azoth had more than one possible meaning in medieval and Renaissance times. While it was often used by alchemists to refer to the element mercury, it also had some more arcane usages. Azoth was described by some to be a panacea, a universal curative that could eliminate illnesses and counteract even the most virulent poisons. It also was used as an alternative name for the philosopher's stone, the legendary object that could create the elixir of life. Others considered Azoth to be the name of a demon or a spirit.

Thus it appears that something significant may have been concealed within the pommel of Paracelsus's sword. Perhaps a chemical capable of curing diseases and acting as an antidote to poison. Or maybe even a demonic entity, bound to serve the will of the person who controlled the sword.

Combative Applications

The exact value of Paracelsus's sword would obviously depend on what exactly lies within the pommel. If azoth is truly a panacea, then it would have a great many uses. Monster hunters could use it to counteract a basilisk's poison, for example. If, on the other hand, Azoth is the name of a demon, then the demon could perhaps be used against one's enemies—or, if it is connected with alchemical knowledge, reveal priceless cosmic secrets to the sword's wielder.

Selected Sources

Jacobi, Jolande, ed., and Norbert Guterman, trans. *Paracelsus*. Princeton, N.J., Princeton University Press, 1995, 248.
An explanation of azoth.

Sharur

History and Description

The Sumerian god Ninurta possessed a sentient mace named Sharur, which means "smasher of thousands." This divine weapon was capable of speech and flight. It would travel the land and return with news, warning Ninurta when a powerful enemy such as the monster Asag approached and presented a threat to the god or his people. Sharur was adept at acquiring information, and could provide its master with information about Asag's origin and powers, preparing him for his deadly foe.

When it came time to do battle, Sharur laid waste to the mountain people who fought for Asag—both when wielded in Ninurta's hands and under its own power, flying and spreading venom and flame upon its master's enemies. As for Asag himself, Ninurta found that he was initially unable to vanquish the monster in combat. Thus Sharur flew to Enlil, Ninurta's father, so that he could form a stratagem that the magical mace would relay to his son. They determined that Asag could be weakened by barrages of rainstorms. Eventually, when the monster had been sufficiently softened up by the torrents of water, Asag used Sharur to slaughter him.

Combative Applications

A divine weapon capable of causing immense crushing damage to one's enemies would be desirable enough, and quite capable of bringing down most monsters. If this was not sufficient, Sharur's ability to exude venom and flame would enable the weapon to

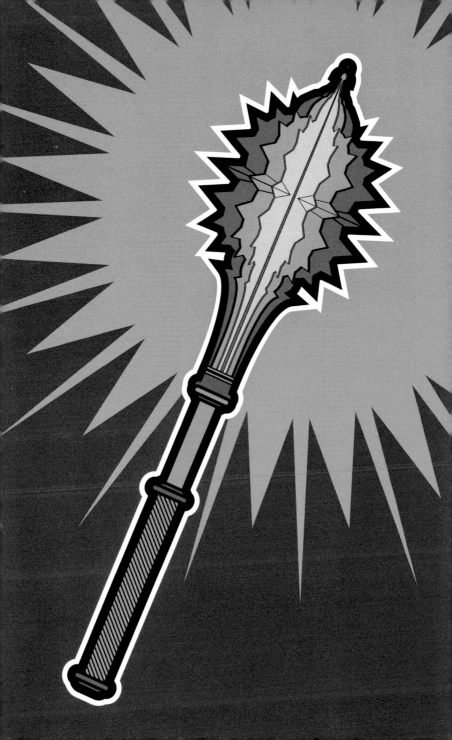

destroy a wide variety of creatures that might be resistant to conventional blows from a weapon. Werewolves and vampires could perhaps not be killed by blows from a mace, but they could certainly be immolated. Sea dragons such as Leviathan, with their impenetrable scales, could possibly shrug off the blows of even an enchanted mace, but venom might be a different matter.

Yet Sharur's true power, the element that perhaps makes it the greatest of all weapons, is the fact that the weapon is sentient. With its ability to fly across the land and report back to its wielder, Sharur would be a perfect scout. It could also give tactical advice when needed, and provide encouragement during difficult battles. Against dangerous monsters whom a hunter may not be able to approach safely—such as the poisonous basilisk—the mace could simply wield itself and crush the creature's skull, while the hunter remained at a distance. Sharur would provide not merely an exceptional weapon, but also a useful ally.

Selected Source

Exploits of Ninurta, **24–69.** Sharur warns Ninurta about Asag; **191–243.** The mace visits Enlil, and returns with a plan to vanquish Asag; **251–64.** Sharur uses venom, flame, and blunt trauma to annihilate Ninurta's enemies; **281–99.** Ninurta slays Asag.

✖ Spear of Destiny ✖
History and Description

As the Crucifixion drew to a close, a Roman centurion stuck his spear into Jesus's side. Blood and water poured from the wound, demonstrating that he was dead (the manner of death on the cross caused fluid to build up in the lungs). Later sources attributed the name Longinus to this Roman, and since then the spear has often been referred to as the Spear of Longinus, or the Spear of Destiny.

The post-Crucifixion history of the weapon is difficult to lay out clearly. Ownership of the relic has been attributed to various famous rulers and conquerors, who allegedly triumphed as long as they possessed it. Unfortunately, it is impossible to know which of these stories are to be believed and which are mere historical fiction. Matters are further obscured by the fact that relics in different locations were declared to be the Spear of Destiny. For example, one fourteenth-century writer noted that in his own time two different objects—one in Paris, one in Constantinople—were each thought to be the Holy Lance.

One of the most notable candidates for the Spear of Destiny is that held in the Hofburg Museum in Vienna. In addition to the ancient and medieval history attributed to it, this lance was also the subject of interesting events in far more recent times. Adolf Hitler is said to have seen the spear while visiting the museum as a young man, and become obsessed with it—sensing the power radiating from the relic. Following his rise to power and his annexation of Austria, Hitler had the spear removed from the museum and sent to Nuremburg. It remained there until the city fell to the Allies, and it came into the hands of General Patton. Shortly afterward, Hitler committed suicide—apparently proving the legends that ruin would shortly follow the loss of the Holy Lance. The spear was returned to the Hofburg Museum, where it resides today.

Combative Applications

The Spear of Destiny is not merely an enchanted weapon but also a holy relic. Hence it may prove extremely effective against the undead, and be a priceless asset on vampire hunts or when battling hordes of zombies. The spear could perhaps also be used to destroy demons, even those who are immune to conventional forms of physical attack.

If the legends are true concerning the power of the spear to grant victory and success to he who possesses it, then its value would of course be even greater. As long as one was careful to maintain control of the weapon, it could potentially set one up for life—ensuring that one's every action was met with a positive result. However, since the power of the spear appears to be tied to its possession, throwing the weapon is not recommended. While it would no doubt destroy the target it was thrown at, the weapon could be lost through such an action—especially if there are other enemies in the immediate area. Since ruin appears to follow the loss of the spear, this could prove disastrous.

Selected Sources

Gospel of John 19.31–37. The biblical account of how Jesus's side was pierced by a Roman centurion's spear while on the cross.

Gospel of Nicodemus (or Acts of Pontius Pilate) 16.7. The Roman centurion is named as Longinus.

Mandeville, Sir John. *The Travels of Sir John Mandeville* **2.** Mandeville, writing in the mid-fourteenth century, claimed that two different rival lances (or at least lance heads) said to be the Spear of Destiny existed at Paris and Constantinople.

Ravenscroft, Trevor. *Spear of Destiny.* **New York: Weiser Books, 1972.** A look at the Second World War and Third Reich from an occult perspective, focusing heavily on the Spear of Destiny.

Sudarsana Chakra
History and Description

As recounted in ancient Indian epics, the Hindu god Vishnu and his avatar Krishna—the physical form the deity took on when he became flesh for the eighth time—used a weapon known as the Sudarsana Chakra. This fabulous artifact was a gift from the fire god Parvaka, who declared that it could be used to slay mortals, demons, or even gods. The weapon was a hoop made of iron and adamant, a legendary metal of incredible hardness. Its outer edge was razor sharp, and would effortlessly slice through any targets it was hurled at. Once its killing was done, the Sudarsana Chakra would magically return to the hand that had thrown it, ready to be hurled once more to inflict further carnage.

Krishna used this chakra to cut down vast armies of demons, thousands at a time. Whenever the lethal disk was flung at the avatar's enemies, the ground would be left littered with their decapitated heads and severed limbs. It was a truly fearsome weapon. Even walls and buildings were no impediment to the Sudarsana Chakra. The weapon was used to destroy the town of Saubha, and cut down the settlement as easily as it sliced through flesh and bone.

In addition to its unstoppable edge, the chakra also could burst into flame. Its divine fire was used to incinerate demons, leaving nothing more than piles of ash in its wake.

Combative Applications

The Sudarsana Chakra would perhaps be the ultimate throwing weapon. It can butcher legions of men or monsters, and bring destruction upon entire towns. It appears that the weapon's flight is entirely guided by its enchantment, meaning that no skill would be required by the wielder. The user would merely have to throw the weapon, then wait for it to eliminate all its targets and return.

The fact that the weapon can burst into flame would make it ideal for immolating whole armies of zombies and the like. It also would be exceptionally useful for dealing with monsters that are immune to most forms of physical attack but can be harmed by fire.

One note of caution, however. If the Sudarsana Chakra can rain down death and destruction on towns and cities, and kill thousands at a time, then it may count as a weapon of mass destruction. Needless to say, nations and international bodies would likely frown on the unauthorized use of such weapons, and this may therefore bring about legal and political difficulties for the wielder.

Selected Source

Mahabharata **1.227.** Parvaka gives Krishna the Sudarsana Chakra; **1.230.** Krishna uses the chakra to slaughter countless demons in battle; **3.22.** The Sudarsana Chakra is described as bursting into flame to incinerate demons, and cutting through the entire town of Saubha; **16.3.** The weapon is described as being made of iron and the hardest adamant.

⊱ Sun Wukong's Staff ⊰
History and Description

Sun Wukong, the legendary Chinese Monkey King, created a
legion of monkeys from his cast-off hairs—which he transformed
into living beings with his considerable magic powers. He trained
this simian battalion in the arts of war, and had them practice
until they were proficient with a wide variety of weapons.
However, while his army was now highly trained and armed with
good-quality weapons, Sun Wukong felt that his own weapon—a
sword he had acquired after killing the Demon King—was far too
clumsy for his liking. Hence he asked his monkey underlings for
advice as to where he might find a more suitable weapon. The
monkeys pointed out that his sword was but a mortal weapon and
therefore not suited to an immortal such as he. They suggested
that he visit the Dragon King at his palace beneath the Eastern
Sea, since the dragons possessed various enchanted artifacts and
were skilled in creating magical arms and armor.

Sun Wukong dived beneath the waves and swam to the Dragon
King's palace. Impressed with the Monkey King's supernatural
abilities, through which he had made his body indestructible, the
dragons gave him a warm welcome. He explained that he was
searching for a weapon, and the Dragon King promised to find
him one. First a fabulous sword was brought out and laid before
Sun Wukong. However, the lord of monkeys said that he was
not skilled in the use of swords. Next a nine-pronged spear
was brought out for him to try. Sun Wukong took it up and
experimented with it, but declared that it was far too light for
him—even though it weighed 3,600 pounds. Next he was offered
a mighty halberd decorated with glyphs that would ward off

harmful spells. This was the heaviest weapon in the Dragon King's palace and weighed 7,200 pounds. Sun Wukong still considered this to be too light for him.

The Dragon King was at a loss, thinking that he had no heavier weapons to set before the Monkey King. Then his wife suggested that they show their guest a piece of iron they had in the treasury that had once been used to hold the universe together. She told him that it had been emitting a rose-colored glow for the past few days, perhaps in anticipation of Sun Wukong's arrival. Skeptical about this object's value as a weapon, but eager to get Sun Wukong out of his home, the Dragon King had him taken to the column of iron. The Monkey King saw that thousands of rays of light were coming from this metal pole, which was twenty feet long and extremely thick. Clearly it was a divine object. Yet he thought that it was a little too long and too thick. He declared that if it was a little shorter and thinner, it would be more suitable. The pole promptly shrank in accordance with his wishes. Its dimensions now made it an ideal staff for him to use. Intrigued by this, Sun Wukong took the staff out of the treasury to obtain a closer look at it. The weapon was formed of black iron, with a gold band at either end. He discovered that there was writing upon it, naming it as the "As-You-Will Gold-Banded Cudgel," and proclaiming its weight to be 13,500 pounds. Sun Wukong had finally found the weapon he would take on his adventures, and use to slay the monsters that stood against him.

After further experimenting with the staff, Sun Wukong found that he could make it as small as a sowing needle and carry it behind his ear. He also could make it as large as a vast tree.

Combative Applications

A staff of variable length would be a rather useful weapon, and tremendously versatile. It could be used as a quarterstaff one moment, then shrunk down and wielded like a club. When not in use, it could be conveniently worn behind the ear or carried in one's pocket.

Obviously the weight of the staff might be a cause for concern—13,500 pounds seems somewhat excessive for even a two-handed weapon. However, this may represent the weight of the staff in the size Sun Wukong originally found it—twenty feet long, and exceptionally thick. When the weapon is reduced in size, the weight also could become more manageable. Furthermore, it appears that the staff may take on the weight the owner desires it to have, meaning that it would become substantially lighter for a human wielder.

Given its ability to grow to an immense size, the staff could be used in various tactical ways. It could double as a battering ram, for example, or be used as a barricade. When fighting an exceptionally strong monster, it may be advisable to drop the staff onto it from a great height, and have it take on a larger size as it falls. Similarly, the staff could be thrown into a monster's mouth, then made to expand—ripping the monster apart.

Selected Source

Wu Cheng'en. *Journey to the West*, Vol. I. Trans. W. J. F. Jenner. Beijing: Foreign Language Press, 2001, 52–61.
Sun Wukong acquires his magical staff from the Dragon King.

⚔ Surt's Sword ⚔
History and Description

Surt, ruler of the fiery realms, will be a pivotal figure during Ragnarok, the Norse apocalypse. It is said that he will come with a flaming sword in his hand that shines brighter than the sun, and proceed to incinerate everything before him. The entire world will burn in his conflagration, and both gods and mortals will perish. The mighty Vanir god Freyr will valiantly attack Surt in an effort to stop this inferno. But Freyr will be poorly armed, having given away his own powerful sword to his servant Skirnir, and therefore not be able to overcome Surt. After a hard battle, the master of the infernal fire will slay Freyr and continue to rage unchecked across the world.

Given these prophecies of end-times, it stands to reason that the flaming sword is currently in Surt's possession—ready to be used in those cataclysmic events of the future. Hence a treasure seeker would have to enter his realm to acquire the weapon, and steal it. Needless to say, such a course of action would be extremely risky, and hardly suitable for the fainthearted. However, if one actually managed to obtain the flaming sword, then in addition to gaining a priceless weapon one would be averting the destruction of mankind—surely a worthy endeavor.

Combative Applications

A flaming sword would be especially effective when hunting certain monsters. Against Hydra, for example, the flames could be used to cauterize the creature's wounds and prevent the growth of new heads. It also would enable the wielder to harm creatures

such as werewolves that are resistant to conventional blades but vulnerable to fire. The sword's alleged brightness could be used to blind one's foes or to scare away beasts. However, the wielder of such a weapon—if the comparisons with the sun are not mere exaggerations—would quite likely be blinded himself if he constantly held the weapon in front of him. This would obviously be rather problematic, and perhaps make the sword more of a trophy than an effective weapon. An especially competent swordsman, capable of fighting blindfolded, could close his eyes before drawing the weapon, and avoid the danger that way.

In the Norse accounts of Ragnarok, it is not precisely clear whether the flames that will burn the world are produced by Surt's flaming sword or by other magical fires at Surt's command. If the former, and the sword can produce such devastating flames, this may be of substantial benefit. Assuming that the flames could be properly controlled and directed, one could destroy entire armies or even cities. Yet a note of caution should be made here. If the flames cannot be properly controlled, then attempting to use the weapon could have catastrophic results. At best it would cause minor fire damage to one's surroundings. At worst it could immolate the entire world and bring about an early apocalypse.

Selected Source

Sturlson, Snorri. *The Prose Edda: Gylfaginning* **4, 51.**
Two descriptions of Surt's sword, and how he will burn the world at Ragnarok.

⚜ Turnus's Helmet ⚜ and Sword

History and Description

When Aeneas came to Italy to found his new kingdom, he encountered a new rival: Turnus. This mighty warrior was described as a second Achilles, and slaughtered many Trojans before he was slain.

Turnus bore two items of note. One was a helmet, atop which was a representation of the Chimera (this particular monster is a lion with a goat's head on its back, and a snake for a tail—see "Chimera" in part I). This Chimera breathed forth flames, the intensity of which would increase depending on how furiously the battle was raging. The second was a sword that could cut through even the divine armor forged by Vulcan—against which mortal blades would break or be deflected.

It is unknown what happened to the sword and helmet following Turnus's death, though it is possible that they are still somewhere in Italy.

Combative Applications

A sword that can cut through even enchanted armor is clearly an excellent weapon to possess. It may be able to cut through the hides of heavily armored dragons, for example, or other such monsters that are otherwise resistant to blades. If it can pierce a piece of divine armor against which regular swords will break, it could also be able to hack through a steel door or other such obstacle.

The helmet also would be a rather impressive piece, though perhaps less useful. There is no indication that the flames can be directed to immolate one's enemies, and there are certain undeniable risks to having a raging fire atop one's head.

Selected Source

Virgil, *Aeneid* **7.785–88.** A description of the helmet; **12.728–41.** Turnus strikes at Aeneas, but the sword he is using breaks. He realizes that he has picked up his charioteer's sword rather than his own, and that a normal weapon is unable to penetrate the divine armor. The clear implication is that his own sword would have been able to pierce Aeneas's corselet.

A Note on the Author

Ibrahim S. Amin graduated from the University of Newcastle, and, later, the University of Manchester. He studied classics and became aware of the monsters that have plagued mankind for millennia, and the fabulous weapons with which to battle them. He currently lives in Manchester. This is his first book.

A Note on the Illustrator

Richard Horne is a designer and illustrator whose work includes record and book covers, Web sites, greetings cards, and newspaper and magazine illustrations. His illustration credits include Daniel Wilson's *How to Survive a Robot Uprising* and *Where's My Jetpack?*, and Conn and Hal Iggulden's *The Dangerous Book for Boys*. Richard is the author of bestselling *101 Things to Do Before You Die* and three more books in the 101 Things series. He lives and works in East London.